D
BATHROOM BOOK
of
OHIO
TRIVIA
Weird, Wacky and Wild

Alicia Adams & Lisa Wojna

Illustrations by Peter Tyler & Roger Garcia

BLUE
BIKE
BOOKS

The Publisher: Blue Bike Books
Website: www.bluebikebooks.com

Library and Archives Canada Cataloguing in Publication

Adams, Alicia, 1967–
    Bathroom book of Ohio trivia / Alicia Adams and Lisa Wojna.

ISBN-13: 978-1-897278-31-4
ISBN-10: 1-897278-31-4

    I. Wojna, Lisa, 1962– II. Title.

F491.6.A33 2007   977.1   C2007-903203-6

Project Director: Nicholle Carrière
Production: Jodene Draven
Illustrations: Peter Tyler, Roger Garcia, Graham Johnson, Roly Wood

We acknowledge the support of the Alberta Foundation for the Arts for our publishing program.

PC: P5

DEDICATION

To veterinarian and author James Herriot, whose wonderful command of the King's English swept me off my feet and charmed me into a lifelong love affair with words.

ACKNOWLEDGMENTS

Contrary to popular opinion, writing is not a solitary occupation. What you can't see as you read this book is the group of people behind the scenes who have supported me and this book with their love and talents. And their willingness to brew several hundred pots of strong coffee for me.

My love and sincere thanks to my husband Rob for his support—computer and otherwise—as well as his encouragement; my son Ryan for offering me his enthusiasm, books and knowledge on Ohio trivia; my daughter Becca for her willingness to tell total strangers how proud she is of her book-writing mom; my mom and dad for their patient support in my effort to become a writer; my sisters for their listening skills and ability to make me laugh; my brother whose love of reading inspired me; my in-laws, extended family and friends for their warm encouragement; and for my dog Ollie, who snored the hours away at my feet while I wrote. He unpretentiously reminded me that the best things in life can be made better with a good nap.

Many thanks also to the Marysville Public Library and the Dublin Branch of the Columbus Metropolitan Library whose books were invaluable. (By the way, sorry about returning them a wee bit late.)

A final heartfelt thanks to you, the reader. When you opened this book, you helped an ordinary girl from Ohio achieve her extraordinary dream of being a writer.

I couldn't have done it without you.

—Alicia Adams

CONTENTS

INTRODUCTION

As an Ohio native I have, naturally, always liked Ohio. But it would take a trip to a foreign country to make me realize why I liked the state so much. A few years ago while touring an ancient Mayan city, my family and I traveled with a guide that had an impressive knowledge of the area. With thoughtful answers and vivid descriptions, he brought a now-vanished civilization to life right before our eyes. To personalize our experience, our guide even showed us an artifact—many generations old and obviously treasured—that had been handed down through his family. His knowledge and enthusiasm turned a typical tourist excursion into a wonderfully alive and enriching afternoon that would be remembered for a long time. And for a moment (or two), I envied him. He lived in a place that had an abundant variety of things to explore.

It was then I suddenly realized I could say the same thing about Ohio. Our state practically bursts with variety. Our history is chock full of presidents, actors and inventors; our landscape runs from swooping Appalachian hills to mellow, rolling farmland to flat city stretches; our culture embraces everyone from the Amish of our agricultural areas to the business moguls of our metropolitan cities to the soccer moms of suburbia. Known by several nicknames, such as the Mother of Presidents, the Heartland of a Nation, the Birthplace of Aviation and the Grand Central Station of the Underground Railroad, Ohio has it all.

But there is more to it than that.

Amid the many offerings of our state are the people who live here. After visiting no fewer than four foreign countries and almost a third of the states within the U.S., I can honestly say that Ohioans are among the nicest people I have ever known. Just as my Mayan tour guide graciously shared a beloved heirloom with a group of curious onlookers, Ohioans cherish their ties with their heritage and welcome the opportunity to share what they have with others.

Now, it is my turn to be the guide. And just like my Mayan counterpart, I want to share with you my knowledge, enthusiasm and love for what lies within Ohio's four borders. Come with me as we explore the colorful, the curious and the wonderful of this state, turning a few hours of your day into what hopefully will be a memorable experience.

> "...Beautiful Ohio, where the golden grain
> Dwarfs the lovely flowers in the summer rain.
> Cities rising high, silhouette the sky.
> Freedom is supreme in this majestic land;
> Mighty factories seem to hum in tune, so grand.
> Beautiful Ohio, thy wonders are in view,
> Land where my dreams all come true!"

–chorus from "Beautiful Ohio," written by Ballard MacDonald

WHAT SETS OHIO APART

Ohio has blended two seemingly opposing points into one factor that make it different from the rest of the nation: a rather unassuming population with a knack for industry and innovation.

A popular catch phrase calls Ohio "the heart of it all." Not just for the shape of the state, but for its central location and many offerings, too. Looking for a city known for its pizzazz, night life and art? Try Columbus and its surrounding areas, located in the middle of the state. Want a quiet rural retreat, maybe something with hills and woods? Look towards the southern part of the state between Cincinnati and Athens. How about a view of water? Try our 300 plus miles of shoreline at the top of the state, gracing the cities and towns from Toledo to Cleveland.

And what about the people? Well, that's the best part. Ohio's agricultural and religious roots have shaped a place with a solid work ethic and strong family values. Its abundant colleges and universities encourage the flow of ideas and innovations. These two elements combined produce a cultural flavor that is uniquely Ohio. Blend that with the natural friendliness of the Midwest and you have a pretty good idea of Ohio's character.

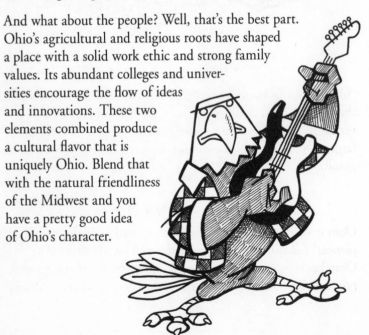

THE NAME GAME

What's in a name?

"Ohio" is an Iroquois word meaning "large or beautiful," words the Iroquois used to describe the "great" Ohio River that traverses the state. While the state's physical geography is far from large, early settlers perhaps found the word fitting because of the grandiose nature of the Ohio's beauty.

Also Known As

Ohio is known as the Buckeye State, named after the trees the pioneers felled in order to clear fields and build cabins. The Ohio buckeye tree is related to the Asiatic horse chestnut and produces a thick, sturdy nut that is dark brown with a tan circle on the top. Native Americans thought it looked like the eye of a male deer, and called the tree "hetuck." White settlers thought it looked like that, too, so they began calling it a "buck eye."

The term "buckeye" was first suggested as a state nickname around 1788, but historians credit the 1840 election of William Henry Harrison as U.S. president for making the name stick. The story goes that his opposition thought him better suited to "sit in a log cabin and drink hard cider" than take his place at the helm of the country. Instead of fighting the image, Harrison's campaign committee used it to their advantage. Harrison became known as "the log cabin candidate" and used a cabin built of buckeye logs as his emblem. Who knows if the buckeye would have been so closely associated with the state had Harrison not won. In any case, from that point forward, the association between the state and tree was made.

DID YOU  KNOW?

It's a bit tough to wrap your tongue around it, but Ohio residents refer to themselves as "Ohioans."

A Higher Power

Mottos typically reflect a belief or ideology embraced by a person or society. Ohio's search for an appropriate motto for its citizens began in the early 1950s and didn't end until October 1, 1959, when the motto "With God All Things Are Possible" was adopted. The idea for this motto, a biblical quote from Matthew 19:26, was submitted by a then 12-year-old James Mastronardo.

Cause for Debate

Ohio's state motto is one of only five state mottos that include the word "God." Not everyone was on board with Ohio's decision to go with James Mastronardo's suggestion of "With God All

Things Are Possible." The American Civil Liberties Union brought the state to court on the matter in 1997, saying the biblical reference "violated the First Amendment to the United States Constitution which guarantees religious freedom and a separation of church and state." Since no specific "God" was mentioned, and therefore no specific religion endorsed, judges ruled that the proposed motto didn't violate the First Amendment.

STATE FLAG AND SEAL

Flying High

Stars, stripes and red, white and blue—Ohio's state flag is nothing if not patriotic. Adopted in 1902, Ohio's flag is called a burgee—a triangular-shaped flag with an indentation that forms two points or tails in the fly. Its design is full of symbolism.

☞ The large blue triangle occupying the left side of the flag represents the state's hills and valleys; the red and white stripes represent the roads and waterways.

☞ The color combination, of course, echoes the red, white, and blue of the Stars and Stripes.

☞ Thirteen stars are grouped to the left side of the large blue triangle, representing the original 13 states.

☞ Ohio was the 17th state to receive statehood, and the four stars grouped near the point of the blue triangle, added to the other 13, represent all 17 states.

☞ The white circle with the red background stands for the "O" in "Ohio."

The Great Seal

Ohio's Great Seal was initially designed in 1847, but like many other state seals, it has evolved into what it is today. Overall, the seal hasn't changed too terribly much. A picturesque scene of a wheat field, complete with a sheaf of wheat and a bundle of 17 arrows, bordered by the Scioto River and green hills in the distance, occupy the center portion. The 17 arrows represent the number of states in the union after Ohio joined. In the background, the sun is rising and 13 rays stretch into the heavens, representing the country's original 13 states. In its first incarnation, a canal boat was pictured on the river, but that was removed in an effort to simplify the design, which was first adopted in 1967 and modified for the last time in 1996.

SYMBOLS AND EMBLEMS

☛ The cardinal was adopted as the state's official bird in 1933.

☛ What better tree to represent the Buckeye State than the Ohio buckeye? It was adopted as the state tree in 1953.

☛ Alliance City was named Ohio's Carnation City in 1959. The city is renowned for the fact that early resident Dr. Levi Lamborn cultivated the Scarlet Carnation in 1886. The red beauty became the official state flower in 1904.

☛ Tomato juice was adopted as Ohio's state beverage in 1965.

☛ Ohio flint is a variety of quartz known for its vibrant colors and used by many in the making of jewelry. It was named the state's official gemstone in 1965.

☛ In 1969, "Beautiful Ohio" was adopted as the official state song. The original words, written by Ballard MacDonald in the very early part of the 20th century, were replaced with words written by Wilbert B. McBride, an attorney from Youngstown. The music to the original was said to be composed by Mary Earl, but that was actually a pseudonym for Robert A. "Bobo" King.

☛ Although it's never been passed into law, the ladybug was designated as Ohio's state insect by resolution in 1975.

☛ During the Ordovician Period (510 to 445 million years ago) Ohio was actually a sea and one of its inhabitants was the Isotelus—an arthropod that is now extinct. The "largest known complete trilobite" was discovered in Montgomery County, and in 1985 the Isotelus was chosen as the state's official invertebrate fossil.

☛ "Hang on Sloopy," by Bert Berns and Wes Farrell, was designated Ohio's official rock song by resolution in 1985. The song was a major hit for the band called The McCoys, who were from Dayton.

☛ The large white trillium, also known as the "wake robin," "snow trillium," "great white trillium" or "white trillium," was adopted as Ohio's official wildflower in 1987.

☛ In 1988, Ohio adopted the white-tailed deer as its state animal. It was chosen for the honor because it's the state's most prolific wild animal, found in all 88 counties. Oddly enough, the deer was once almost hunted to extinction in Ohio, but new regulations and consideration for its habitat gave it room for a comeback. Today there are about 450,000 deer in the state.

☛ The black racer snake was chosen as Ohio's state reptile in 1995.

☛ Blaine Hill Bridge was named the state's official Bicentennial Bridge in 2002. Build in Belmont county in 1828, it's the state's oldest bridge.

DID YOU KNOW?

What do James Abram Garfield, Ulysses Simpson Grant, Warren G. Harding, Benjamin Harrison, William Henry Harrison, Rutherford B. Hayes, William McKinley and William Howard Taft all have in common? They were all presidents and they all, with the exception of Harrison, who moved to the state later in life, were born in Ohio. It's because of this fact that Ohio has earned the nickname "Mother of Presidents."

AND THE SURVEY SAYS...

Up Against the Rest

Ever wonder where Ohio sits when it comes to other states in the country? Here are just a few points for you to ponder, based on 2006 High Beam survey results:

☛ Ohio was ranked the 37th most livable state, down from a 2005 ranking of 32nd.

☛ Ohio came in 24th when it came to the healthiest state rankings, up two spots from 2005's 26th spot.

☛ It may be surprising to some, but Ohio ranks as the 23rd most dangerous state to live in, mirroring its 2005 ranking.

☛ When it comes to the smartest state rankings, Ohio slipped drastically from the 20th position in 2005 to its current ranking of 34th.

DID YOU KNOW?

Tomato juice was chosen as the state's official beverage because Ohio leads the entire country in the production of that particular drink.

WEATHERING THE WEATHER

"You know you're in Ohio if you've ever had to switch from the furnace heat to the air conditioning in the same day."
—Ohio saying

Four Seasons in One Day

Planning an Ohio trip? Better pack the way the Scouts do—be prepared. There's an old saying that goes something like this: "If you don't like the weather, just wait a few minutes. It'll change." As strange as it seems, it's true. No matter where in Ohio you are, chances are you're going to see at least two different weather events on any given day. It always pays to have two essentials on hand when you travel: an umbrella and a jacket. If you're traveling from November to March, it never hurts to have a snow/ice scraper in your car, either.

A Continental Climate

Ohio, located between 38 and 42 degrees north latitude and at low elevations, has a continental climate. Ohioans experience four distinct seasons with large temperature fluctuations and frequent precipitation. The prevailing winds are from the west, which leads to frequent weather changes (thus the saying). Mostly the summers are warm, with average temperatures around 85.8°F, though they sometimes soar into the 90s. Humidity can sometimes be challenging in the southern portions of the state, and thunderstorms and tornadoes are common. Winters in Ohio's northern latitudes are at times cooler than the average of 15.5°F experienced by the rest of the state, and the area bordering Lake Erie has heavier snowfalls, experiencing about 40 inches a year. Central portions of Ohio can expect about 30 inches of snowfall each year whereas the southern portion recieves about 20 inches.

WEATHER EXTREMES

Hot Spot

Ohio's highest temperature was recorded in Gallipolis on July 21, 1934. It was a blistering 113°F degrees that day.

Cold Spot

The coldest temperature recorded in Ohio was in Milligan. On February 10, 1899, it was a frigid -39°F.

Extreme Weather Moments

When it comes to extreme weather, Ohio has had its share. Blizzards, heat waves, tornadoes and even hurricanes have all had a role in the state's weather history, landing entries in the history books for lives lost, damage inflicted and records broken. What follows are some of the worst of the worst.

☞ Hurricanes are usually associated with coastal areas, but in November 1913, a weather system formed over the Great Lakes region that rapidly strengthened into a full-blown hurricane. Called by several names, such as the "Big Blow," the "Freshwater Fury" and the "White Hurricane" and lasting for almost six days, this storm generated waves over three stories tall and packed walloping winds that reached speeds of 145 miles per hour. An inadequate communications system and deceiving lulls in the storm contributed to the worst natural disaster in the Great Lakes' history. Forty-two ships were lost at sea or stranded on the shore and at least 270 sailors lost their lives. It was one of the worst weather events ever visited upon Cleveland in terms of wind, snow and ice. The final financial tally for Ohio alone was estimated at well over $4 million.

☞ On Friday, July 28, 2006, after six days of heavy rain throughout Lake County, then Governor Bob Taft declared a state of emergency. During a 12-hour period on July 22 alone, more than 9 inches of rain fell, flooding nearby Ashtabula County and soaking Geauga and Lake Counties. In the end, most of the damage—113 buildings destroyed, more than 300 additional buildings damaged to a lesser degree—occurred in Lake County.

☞ While most wind damage in Ohio is the result of tornadoes, occasionally there are times when highs winds occur without a tornado tagging along. These wind storms are known as microbursts, and while their name implies something little, there's nothing small about them. In 1915, a fierce thunderstorm descended upon Cincinnati in the evening hours of July 7 and produced a microburst that was nothing short of catastrophic. Winds tore the sides and roofs off stone and brick buildings; houses, apartments, and commercial buildings collapsed into their foundations. Cars were blown more than 200 feet from their original parking spots and entire trains were blown off their tracks. Over 15 people died when their boats overturned on the Ohio River. More than $1 million of property damaged occurred during this microburst, and the final death toll for the city was 38.

☞ Heavy rain caused flooding on September 19, 2004. While only 21 counties were initially affected, fewer than in February 2005, more than $33 million in damages was reported.

☞ The entire state of Ohio alternately baked and broiled in the summer of 1934. The hottest summer on record ever, the average temperature was 75.7°F, a full 5° degrees above normal. Several times throughout the months of June, July and August the temperature soared into the triple digits and stayed there for days, taking its toll on the young, the elderly and the weak. During one week alone, over 160 deaths were reported, the direct result of the oppressive heat.

☞ Storms, flooding and a tornado wracked up more than $132 million in damages throughout 12 counties on August 1, 2003.

☞ Snow and ice caused almost $41 million in damages throughout 30 Ohio counties on March 14, 2003.

☞ The deepest snowstorm in Ohio's history occurred during Thanksgiving weekend in 1950. An intense snowstorm lingered over the state from November 23 through November 27, blanketing the entire state with an average of just under a foot of snow, with several communities receiving almost three feet. When the winds picked up speed to 60 miles per hour, snow drifts commonly reached 25 feet deep. Many buildings collapsed under the weight of the snow.

☞ On February 15, 2005, severe winter storms caused flooding in 32 counties throughout Ohio. By the end of March, 63 counties had been affected by the storms and were eligible for help from the Federal Emergency Management

Agency (FEMA). A total of $7.7 million in damages was
reported.

☛ Twenty-three counties were peppered with severe winds,
tornadoes and rains that caused flash floods and $56 mil-
lion in damages on June 30, 1998.

☛ Almost a year earlier, on March 4, 1997, about $68 million
in damages were caused to 16 counties by flash flooding on
the Ohio River.

☛ Flooding back in March and April of 1913 caused $143
million in damages state-wide and 467 deaths. This flood
is listed on the U.S. Significant Floods of the 20th Century.

Shadyside Flood

When weather forecasters called for more rain on June 14, 1990,
residents of Shadyside cringed. They were still trying to dry out
from a very wet May. However, this time the weather would be
different—in a deadly way. It started raining as predicted, but
around 7:30 p.m. the weather took a turn for the worse. The
rain became torrential, dumping almost six inches on Shadyside
within three and half hours. This enormous rainfall caused the
nearby creeks of Wegee and Pipe to overflow their banks and
join together, creating a wall of water over six feet high.

This wall came crashing through town around midnight,
seemingly out of nowhere, ripping entire brick houses from
their foundations, tearing whole sides off multi-story buildings
and snatching trailer homes from their parks. The debris from
the town and surrounding area was carried 30 miles down-
stream until it finally came to a stop at Hannibal Dam, forming
a field of wreckage that covered 15 acres. By the time it was over,
26 people had been swept away to their deaths, 80 homes had
been destroyed and more than 250 buildings had been damaged.

LAY OF THE LAND

By the Numbers

Ohio is the 34th largest state in the nation, covering 44,825 square miles and measuring 220 miles from north to south and 220 miles from east to west. Most of that area, or 40,953 square miles, is land and 3875 square miles is covered by water.

Largest County

While many Ohio counties measure about 440 square miles, when it comes to size, Ashtabula County is the largest hands down, measuring 711 square miles.

The Big Picture

The Ohio state landscape is primarily made up of rolling hills and prairie flatlands, which can be divided into the following main regions: the Great Lakes Plains (also known as the Huron-Erie Lake Plains), the Till Plains, the Appalachian Plateaus and the Glaciated Allegheny Plateaus, the Bluegrass Region and the Lake Erie Shoreline.

Highs and Lows

With a geography that alternates between flat plains and undulating meadows, Ohio doesn't have extreme high and low elevations. The state's mean elevation is about 850 feet above sea level. Ohio's highest point is Campbell Hill, at an elevation of 1549 feet, and its lowest point is the Ohio River at 455 feet above sea level.

Front and Centre

Travel about 25 miles northeast of Columbus City, in Delaware County, and you'll find yourself in the geographic centre of Ohio.

State Rivers

Overall, Ohio has a fairly small percentage of land covered in water. Still, there are several rivers of considerable importance. The Maumee River, Sandusky River, Cuyahoga River and Mahoning River are all located in the northern portion of the state and drain into the Atlantic Ocean via the Great Lakes Waterway. The Great Miami River, Little Miami River, Scioto River, Hocking River and Muskingum River are located in the south and drain southward into the Gulf of Mexico via the Ohio and Mississippi Rivers.

Major Lakes

Ohio boasts only two main lakes: Lake Erie and Grand Lake St. Marys—a manmade lake constructed in the 1800s as a reservoir for a canal system. Boating, diving and other water sports might be a tad difficult on Grand Lake St. Marys. Although the lake covers an area of 13,055 acres, its deepest point measures a scant 7 feet.

Glorious Green

About 30 percent of Ohio is covered in forest. And the state boasts 20 state forests covering more than 183,000 acres of land and another 74 state parks covering more than 204,000 acres.

Love Thy Neighbor

Ohio isn't a state that's short on neighbors. Flanking its borders, clockwise from north, are Michigan, Pennsylvania, West Virginia, Kentucky and Indiana. Lake Erie's proximity to the state affects climate to a degree—the state's snow belt borders the southern portion of the lake.

Among Ohio's 74 state parks is the 17,229 acre Salt Fork State Park in Lore, Ohio's largest state park.

ODD OHIO GEOLOGY

Blue Hole of Castalia

Regarded by the Wyandot people as a place with great healing powers, the artesian spring known as the Blue Hole of Castalia is now a state fish hatchery. That fact doesn't dull its sparkling mystery, though. This pond-sized spring is well fed from several and mostly unknown underground sources of water; an estimated 7519 gallons a minute flow from it into Lake Erie. Unaffected by floods and drought, the water remains a constant 48°F year-round and is completely without oxygen content, making it crystal clear. The presence of lime, soda, magnesium and iron give it the blue color it is famed for. Divers have yet to locate the bottom of this Ohio anomaly, so for now the secrets of the Blue Hole of Castalia will remain hidden away within its clear blue depths.

Glacial Grooves

About 18,000 years ago, a glacier hundreds of feet thick retreated over the land now known as Ohio. In the process, the ice scoured grooves into the local limestone bedrock leaving a trough 400 feet long, 35 feet wide and 10 feet high in its wake. The north shore of Kelly's Island displays the largest easily accessible grooves in the world. Walking along the grooves, one can view marine fossils that are 350 to 400 million years old.

Buckeye Lake Cranberry Bog

A little bit of the Ice Age still thrives in Licking County. An advancing glacier from the north pushed a belt of forest into Ohio 11,000 years ago, creating a swamp where the cold-loving flora thrives to this day. In the 1830s, canal construction caused a large bog mat to break loose and float away from the marsh; today it is still the only floating cranberry island in the world.

Pass the Salt, Please, and Throw Some On the Road As Well

Ohio possesses a cornucopia of sodium chloride—enough to last the nation for the next 32,000 years, give or take a few. Brine mines, more commonly known as salt mines, were formed by the sea water that covered the state 400 million years ago. An average of 4.1 million tons is mined from tunnels 2000 feet below Lake Erie; 40 percent goes to industry, 55 percent is used for ice control and 5 percent is shaken onto America's food.

NUMBER ONE POLLUTER

What Stinks?

With the capital city of Columbus noted for its cleanliness, and the surrounding areas prettily colored with golden grain fields and lush green forests and grass, you might think that Ohio has no problems keeping its environment healthy. Unfortunately, that's not the case.

According to the U.S. Environmental Protection Agency, Ohio released more chemicals into the air from industry smokestacks and similar devices than any other state between the years 1998 and 2003. When comparing overall releases to the environment, Ohio came in fourth in the nation.

Ohio is one of the country's most industrialized states, and it has an "F" on its environmental report card to show for it.

ENVIRONMENT

Depleting Forests

Of the almost 26.1 million acres of land that make up Ohio, about 25 million acres were originally forest. Clearing land for agriculture and communities depleted all but 1.6 million acres of forest by 1940. But shortly thereafter a new appreciation for protecting natural forests and even in rebuilding the state's woodland took hold, and forested land grew to 7.9 million acres by 1996. Today, Ohio State University has identified about 150 tree varieties native to Ohio. Of those there are at least 30 varieties of hawthorn, 14 oak, 6 hickory and 6 ash, 7 maple and 15 willow species.

DID YOU  KNOW?

The Cuyahoga River in Cleveland actually caught on fire in 1969. An oil slick covering the surface of the water erupted when sparks from a passing train landed on it. Sadly, it wasn't the first time the river went up in flames. It happened a total of 10 times before the 1969 fire.

Cleaning Up the Mess

In spite of the state's dubious honor of being the number one polluter in the nation, slow progress is being made to decrease pollution levels. While the 2003 data still places Ohio at the top of the list, the numbers have progressively gone down in recent years.

Big and Black

Until it began draining back in the mid-1800s, what was known as the Great Black Swamp covered much of the state's north-western portion. Today, the 321-acre Goll Woods State Nature Preserve near Archbold protects many of Ohio's largest trees, oaks between 200 and 400 years old, wildflowers and foliage that collectively represent the state's most pristine forest.

ANIMAL FACTS

Species at Risk

The number of species listed as endangered or threatened by the Ohio Department of Natural Resources Division of Wildlife is shocking. In 2003, the species list included 5 mammals (including the black bear, which we all think is everywhere); 19 birds; 5 reptiles; 5 amphibians; 24 fish; 24 mollusks; 13 dragonflies; 2 damselflies; 3 caddisflies, 2 mayflies; 1 midge; 8 butterflies; 14 moths; 3 pointed sallow; and 3 beetles. Together, that's a staggering 123 species. It definitely makes one think, doesn't it?

Watch Your Step

Heads up to everyone who, like me, is petrified of snakes. Apparently the sleek, black rat snake can be found in most parts of the state. And it's no small creature either. It typically grows between four and six feet in length, but some specimens have been found measuring eight very long feet, making this the biggest creature of its kind in Ohio. Still, because of the snake's propensity to do away with pesky rodents, folks at the Ohio Department of Natural Resources have dubbed the black rat snake "one of Ohio's most beneficial and splendid reptile assets."

DID YOU  KNOW?

In 1951, a mischievous young member of the Lazarus family (of Columbus-based department store fame) slipped a pocketful of lizards past customs at the airport while returning from vacation in Milan, Italy. He let them loose in his neighborhood, where they flourished and are now considered a native species. They are commonly known as wall lizards or Lazarus lizards.

Gobble, Gobble, Gone?

It wasn't an intentional plan, but by 1904 the once prolific wild turkey had vanished from Ohio. Their extinction from the state appeared to be caused by depleted forest land. In an effort to repopulate the species, the Ohio Division of Wildlife began reintroducing the birds into the wild. Initial attempts failed, largely because the birds being released were raised in captivity. So, in the late 1950s, wild birds from other states were transported to Ohio and today these feathered fowl can be found in all 88 counties, growing to an adult weight of as much as 24 pounds—the perfect size for Thanksgiving dinner!

DID YOU KNOW?

There are 13 species of bats recorded by Ohio's Division of Wildlife as living in Ohio. Among them is the very rare Indiana bat, which is listed on the endangered species list for the state and the country.

Making Friends

For Ohioans living along Lake Erie, living with water snakes is just part of everyday life. They're not poisonous, but they do bite and they can overrun your property. Ohio's wildlife department suggests methods of dealing with them that include removing them by using a cloth to cover the head of the snake ("to protect yourself from bites and flying feces"); giving snakes their own habitat in your yard by building a brush pile on the beach away from where you swim; and stomping on the dock to frighten possible snakes away. The wildlife department also points out another very important point—if you've got snakes, you've likely got mice or other pesky rodents, so the snakes are a handy and free form of rodent control. Unfortunately, in 2003, the Lake Erie water snake was added to Ohio's Endangered Species List.

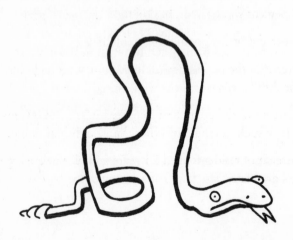

POPULATION INFORMATION

"A right sturdy set of fellows."

–Herman Melville, on the residents of the Ohio Valley

First Inhabitants

The original inhabitants of Ohio were Native Americans from the Erie, Kickapoo and Shawnee tribes. As Europeans began settling the area, other native tribes followed; the Delaware, Miami, Ottawa, Ohio Senecca (Mingo) and Wyandot tribes. But during the 1800s, most Native Americans were forced out of the state, and today there is only one federally recognized native tribe in Ohio, the Shawnee Nation, United Remnant Band.

Population at a Glance

According to the 2005 census estimates:

☛ 6.4 percent of Ohio's population was under five years old;

☛ 24.1 percent was under 18;

☛ 13.3 percent was 65 years and older;

☛ 51.3 percent of the population was female;

☛ 3 percent of the population claimed to be of foreign birth in the 2000 Census;

☛ 6.1 percent of the population reported in the 2000 Census that they spoke a language other than English at home;

☛ 83 percent of residents aged 25 years and older were high school graduates;

☛ 21.1 percent of residents aged 25 years and older had a Bachelor's degree or higher;

☛ 1,909,489 Ohioans aged five and older reported having a disability;

☛ The average home in Ohio costs $103,700.

Major Cities

Based on 2005 population estimates from the U.S. Census Bureau, Ohio's three major cities are Columbus, Cleveland and Cincinnati.

☛ Columbus is the state's capital and also the most populated city with 730,657 residents. Cleveland comes in second with 452,208 residents.

☛ Cincinnati is third with a population of 308,728.

☛ Toledo trails close behind Cincinnati with 301,285 residents, followed by Akron (210,795), Dayton (158,873), Parma (82,837), Youngstown (81,469), Canton (79,478) and Lorain (67,820), rounding out Ohio's top 10 cities.

County Claim

The most populated county in Ohio, though smaller in landmass than most, is Cuyahoga County. Census estimates from 2005 put 1,335,317 residents living there.

Population by State
(July 2005 Estimates)

Ranking	State	Population
1	California	36,132,147
2	Texas	22,859,968
3	New York	19,227,088
7	Ohio	11,464,042
10	New Jersey	8,717,925
15	Indiana	6,271,973
20	Wisconsin	5,536,201
30	Iowa	2,966,334
40	Maine	1,321,505
50	Washington, D.C.	563,523[1]

1 If Washington D.C. were a state, its rank by population would be 50th, just ahead of Wyoming.

Population per Square Mile
(2000 Estimates)

State	Population
Washington, D.C.	9378
New Jersey	1134.5
Massachusetts	809.8
Ohio	253.3
Washington	88.6
Alaska	1.1

Ohio Population Through the Years

Year	Population	Density per square mile
1800	5,365	1.00
1820	581,434	12.97
1840	1,519,467	33.89
1860	2,339,511	52.19
1880	3,198,062	71.35
1900	4,157,545	92.75
1920	5,759,394	128.49
1940	6,907,612	154.10
1960	9,706,397	216.54
1980	10,797,630	240.88
2000	11,353,140	253.3
2006 (estimates)	11,478,006	256.06

ETHNIC DIVERSITY

Diversity, or Lack Thereof

According to U.S. Census estimates for 2005, 85 percent of Ohio's population is Caucasian, 11.9 percent is African American, 2.3 percent is Latino, 1.4 percent is Asian and 1.3 percent declares itself of mixed heritage of two or more ethnic backgrounds.

Only 0.2 percent of Native Americans or Native Alaskans call Ohio home.

Population by Race
(2005 Estimates)

Race	Population
White	9,759,187
African American	1,368,406
Native American	25,313
Asian	163,726
Two or more races	121,760

Population by Ethnicity
(2004 Estimates)

Ethnic Background	Percentage of population
German	25.2
Irish	12.7
African American	11.5
English	9.2
American	8.5
Italian	6.0

OUTSTANDING OHIO

With a total population of 11,478,006, Ohio is the seventh-most populated state in the United States. Its population represents 3.8 percent of the 229,398,484 people who call the country home.

POPULATION FUN FACTS

☛ Ohio's period of most rapid growth occurred between 1950 and 1960. During that time the state's population increased by 22 percent or 1.8 million residents.

☛ Because of the state's birth and death rates, Ohio's population grows by about 115 residents each day.

☛ About 64 people move out of Ohio each day.

☛ The median age of Ohioans is 36.2 years.

☛ Based on 2000 figures, the average life expectancy in Ohio is 76.4 years. Women in Ohio generally live longer, with a life expectancy of about 78.7 years, whereas men in Ohio can expect to make it to 73.8 years.

☛ Only one in five Ohioans live in rural areas.

☛ The combined population of Cincinnati, Cleveland and Columbus is equivalent to almost half the state's population.

☛ Ohioans are getting older. According to the 2000 Census, every day 14 residents reach the golden age of 65 years. Census predictions are that by 2012, 119 residents a day will be hitting that milestone.

☛ Ohio has a population of more than 35,000 Amish, many of whom reside in Holmes, Wayne and Tuscarawas counties. This represents the largest Amish population in the world.

HEY BABY, WHAT'S YOUR NAME?

Baby Names

Based on information culled from Social Security care applications to February 2006, Ohio mirrors much of the country when it comes to the top five favorite baby names. For girls, Emma, Madison, Olivia, Emily and Ava rounded out the top five picks, while Jacob, Andrew, Ethan, Michael and Logan were the top five boys' names. The five most popular boys' and girls' names were similar in most states, although their ranking may have been different, but 19 other states joined Ohio in choosing Jacob for the number one baby boy name, and 19 other states agreed with Ohio's first pick of Emma for baby girls.

UNIQUE PLACES

The Wilds

It's not the usual assortment of Ohio wildlife: camels, rhinos, zebras and giraffes. And it's not the usual type of setting for such animals: all of them are living together in a strip mine. Yep, that's right—a strip mine. Welcome to The Wilds, North America's largest preserve for endangered species. The 10,000 acres that form The Wilds used to be an open strip mine in all of its raw ugliness. American Electric Power reclaimed the land and then gave it as a gift to the public. Located in Cumberland, the preserve holds animals from all around the world and is sectioned off in one of three quadrants: African, Asian and North American. Visitors observe them from buses that give them a chance to get a bit closer to the exotic species.

Amish Country

This unique place is not just in one area but in four. Holmes, Wayne, Tuscarawas and Stark counties are home to Ohio's largest Amish communities. The Amish live a simple, agriculturally based lifestyle and shun the use of cars and electricity because of their potential for disrupting their lifestyle.

The trademark horses and black buggies are seen everywhere in these areas. Also located in these parts are stores and more stores: everything from shops that supply non-electric appliances and equipment to merchants specializing in Amish foods and handmade items. While the Amish welcome the outside world to enjoy the fruits of their lifestyle, they are careful to make sure the commercial scene doesn't overwhelm their communities. Plan a whole day to browse this beautiful and unique part of Ohio, but make sure it's not Sunday because that's the Amish day of rest.

DID YOU  KNOW?

There are about 15 Swiss cheese factories in the Amish area of Sugarcreek. It's a heritage that dates back to Jacob Steiner, who was making cheese by 1833. Today, area factories produce an estimated 10 million pounds of the Swiss favorite each year, a main contributor to Ohio's reputation as the biggest Swiss cheese producer in the country.

Tecumseh!

A live military cannon explodes off to your right. A thunderous herd of galloping horses comes rounding the corner from your left. Are you at a Civil War reenactment? No. You're experiencing the live outdoor drama known as *Tecumseh!*

Recounting the life of Shawnee Indian leader Tecumseh every summer, this professional theater production is set in the hills of Appalachia, not far from Chillicothe, in the 1800 seat amphitheater at Sugarloaf Mountain. The play was written by Emmy award-winning playwright Allan W. Eckert, the music scored by The London Symphony Orchestra and the narration sequences recorded by Canadian-born Native actor Graham Greene. This production has garnered international acclaim in its 35-year history and has been seen by over 2 million people.

The Roller Coaster Capital of the World

Cedar Point, an amusement park located by Lake Erie in Sandusky, is no stranger to fame, attracting more than 3 million visitors each year. It's ranked number one in the world for amusement parks and is the second-oldest amusement park in America. Originally used for hunting and fishing, the peninsula was developed in 1870 to hold a beer garden and a public beach. Guests found the area so attractive that they demanded additional leisure activities. In 1892, the roller coaster legacy began

when the first roller coaster, the Switchback Railway, was constructed. Since then, Cedar Point has never looked back. It now has 68 rides and currently holds the world record for most roller coasters—17 of them. It's also ranked number three in the world for having the friendliest staff, some of whom have found fame and fortune for themselves, most notably Arsenio Hall and Knute Rockne.

ROADSIDE ATTRACTIONS

Advertisement Extraordinaire!

If you happen to find yourself driving along State Route 16 in Newark and pass by the Longaberger Company headquarters, you might find it hard to keep your eyes on the road. That's because the company's corporate office is designed in the shape of a giant woven basket. The idea was the brainchild of Dave Longaberger, son of company founder J.W. Longaberger. His father got into the basket-making industry in 1919 and, following the Depression, purchased the Dresden Basket Factory. Dave took over his father's company in 1976 and it was his idea to build a company headquarters in the shape of the factory's biggest seller, the Medium Market Basket. His dream was finally realized when it opened for business on December 17, 1997.

DID YOU KNOW?

Longaberger baskets were used as decoration on the set of the popular television sitcom *Friends*.

Ode to the Politician

If you're in Cleveland traveling down East 66th and Chester Avenue, you might happen upon an odd piece of public sculpture, a 40 foot by 40 foot by 35 foot monstrosity made of steel, fiberglass, rope and assorted discarded items, such as the odd television set or two. Called *The Politician: A Toy*, it was built by Billy Lawless in 1995. The moving, noise-making sculpture is meant as a visual reflection of politicians everywhere, right down to the shovel (for ground-breaking ceremonies), a bow tie and a wagon handle (to easily follow the herd). Lawless has other controversial pieces on display in Cleveland, one of the most notable being a neon sign on Pearl Road announcing "Atomic Playground Ahead," and inviting children to "Ride the Big One."

National First Ladies Library

With the guys always seeming to get all the attention with their museums, it was about time the ladies had a crack at it. Located in downtown Canton, the National First Ladies Library is a national archive devoted to First Ladies and other notable women in history. It is a physical educational facility, a multimedia repository and an electronic virtual library wrapped up into one location. There is no other library like this one in the world.

Some firsts from Ohio's First Ladies:

☛ Dolly Madison, wife of President James Madison, coined the term "First Lady."

☛ Lucy Webb Hayes, wife of President Rutherford B. Hayes, was the first First Lady with a college diploma. She also started the White House Easter Egg Roll.

☛ Helen "Nellie" Taft is the only U.S. president's wife buried in Arlington National Cemetery; she is also responsible for the cherry trees in Washington, D.C.

☛ At age 65, Anna Symes Harrison was the oldest woman to become First Lady. She would also become the first Presidential widow.

Welcome to Dreamsville

During the 1940s, the Dennison Railroad Station became the third-largest canteen in the country, welcoming military men and women with free food, hot coffee and a smile as they passed their way to and from World War II. This service was run by the Salvation Army Servicemen's Canteen and became a fond memory of comfort and kindness for the half a million soldiers it served, earning its nickname of "Dreamsville, Ohio." It is now a fully restored working railroad as well as a railroad museum.

Free For All

It measures 28 feet tall and 48 feet long and it graces Cleveland's downtown area. If you've been there you likely know what I'm talking about. Cleveland boasts the "World's Largest Rubber Stamp." Originally commissioned as a mascot for Standard Oil, soon after it was created, it found itself abandoned in an Indiana warehouse. Eventually the company, which changed its name to Amoco after a business merger, donated the stamp to the city. Initially Cleveland refused the offer, reasoning the city didn't have money in the coffers for something as frivolous as installing and maintaining a giant rubber stamp. When Amoco offered to do the job pro bono, the city relented. Appropriately enough, the free gift bears the word "FREE" on its stamp.

Remembering a Tragedy

Drive along Cardington Road in Marion and you'll likely notice four limestone slabs surrounding a marble slab that covers the remains of John Grimm. Sadly, on October 6, 1833, at the age of 52 years, the man was struck by a falling tree and died at this very spot. Exactly why he's buried there is a mystery.

Graveyard Hopping

If you're into touring graveyards, check out the Marion Cemetery on Delaware Avenue. A 5200-pound, polished granite ball has been rotating on a pedestal there for more than 100 years. *Ripley's Believe It or Not* apparently featured the mystery as far back as 1929.

Don't Bring Your Newspaper

If you ever need to use the public restroom while in Yellow Springs, you are in for a treat. Two local artists, Nancy Mellon and Corrine Bayraktarolgu, have come up with a fresh way to display local artists' work. A few years ago, they needed a place that had easy access and high traffic, a place guaranteed to make people look. But where? That's when they had a brainstorm. Why not the bathroom? That's when The Chamber Pot Gallery was born. Located inside a replica 1880 train station, the gallery showcases paintings by various artists and enjoys popularity with both townsfolk and tourists alike. Admission is free and everyone is welcome to enjoy a little culture as they answer nature's call.

Heavenly Help?

Back in 2004, members of Munroe's Solid Rock Church pondered how they could get their message that "Jesus Saves" out to passing motorists. After a lot of prayer, they sought the help of designer Brad Coriel and artist James Lynch and decided to build the mother of all Jesus statues. Standing 62 feet tall and weighing about 16,000 pounds, the King of Kings statue reaches arms upward and, facing Interstate 75, can't help but give folks something to think about, or at least to stare at.

The Boy and the Boot

Apparently, more than one person has attempted to retrace the history behind the "boy and the boot" statues and itemize how many of these oddities exist in public places (at least 24, according to one source). Ohio claims two such sculptures. The original zinc statue, imported from Baden, Germany in 1876, is located in the lobby of Sandusky City Hall, and a bronze replica of this statue is located in Sandusky's Washington Park.

Mac-n-Cheese Castles?

It sounds like Mac-n-Cheese, but the native name for this beautiful area in Logan County is mac-o-chee, meaning "rolling hills." It was here that the Piatt brothers Abram and Don built their Piatt Castles. Why pick rural Logan County to build these architectural oddities? Their father Benjamin Piatt acquired about 1700 acres of land in the area after fighting in the War of 1812. With plenty of land to pass around, he bestowed equal shares on his sons, and they decided to use it to build themselves each a castle roughly one mile apart.

Abram's Castle Piatt Mac-A-Cheek was the first built. He apparently built it to last because this Gothic three-story home (with its five-story watch tower) has limestone walls two feet thick. Beautiful woodwork done in ash, pine and walnut adorns the interior, as do frescoes on the ceilings. Interesting artifacts include Revolutionary War period wardrobes and original furnishings from the 1800s.

His brother Don's Castle Mac-O-Chee was constructed in a Flemish style with limestone wrapping around part of it. Don's castle also contains fine examples of woodworking and beautifully frescoed walls and ceilings.

The castles remain in the Piatt family to this day and are open to visitors.

Man of Steel

A ghostly figure of a hooded metal man holding a long-handled ladle stands at the junction of Highway 22 and Highway 7 in Steubenville. The statue was built by Ohio Valley Steelworkers in 1989 and represents the steel industry, which has been a backbone of the Steubenville economy for generations.

House of Trash

Candy Slaughter is smitten with the three Rs: reduce, reuse and recycle, especially the last two. In fact, she likes reducing and reusing so much that she hand-built a 1650 square foot house from tires, pop cans and bottles. This eco-friendly house uses various self-sustaining technologies, so it does not generate utility bills, yet still provides the same comforts as any modern home. Located in Philo, at Blue Rock Station, you can take a tour and see for yourself the incredible house that garbage made.

Roadside Memorial

If this doesn't encourage safer driving, nothing will. Back on August 20, 1835, a stagecoach driver was traveling a little too quickly along a notorious stretch of road near Norwich, now called Dead Man's Curve. Passenger Christopher C. Baldwin, a librarian with the American Antiquarian Society in Worchester, Massachusetts, was killed when the stagecoach overturned, pinning him underneath. The accident made him the state's first official traffic fatality, and the spot was marked with a memorial plaque in 1925 by area historian Rollin Allen.

SMALL TOWN ODDITIES

Hamilton Hollows?

Back in 1818, Captain John Cleves Symmes posited that the earth was made up of an 800-mile thick crust, beyond which it was hollow. Symmes further reasoned that the inner earth was even inhabitable. While the "Hollow Earth" theory, as it came to be known, didn't garner a lot of serious interest in the scientific community, some scholars have played with the idea of testing the theory, and it has made great fodder for science-fiction writers. Either way, at his death in 1829, Symmes was buried in Hamilton's Symmes Park, and in the 1840s his son erected a monument to his father and his theory at the park, located on Sycamore Street.

Lighting the Way

Ashville boasts the "world's oldest traffic light." The light is typically kept at the town's museum, but every July 4th it's hung over the entrance to the town's community park.

DID YOU KNOW?

John Curtis Holmes hails from Ashville. Whether you know him or not may depend on your taste in movies. He's considered by some the "biggest actor in the history of the adult film industry." Holmes' career began to decline in the late 70s due to drug abuse, and in 1981 he was arrested and tried for the gruesome Wonderland murders in Los Angeles, California. He was later aquitted, but his life never really returned to its former fame. He died of AIDS in 1988. The films *Boogie Nights* starring Mark Wahlberg and *Wonderland* starring Val Kilmer are based on his life.

Stars and Stripes

Lancaster was home to the young Robert Heft. When he was just a high school student, in 1958, he designed the country's 50-star flag as a school project but received only a "B–" for his efforts. His design was accepted by Congress in 1959 between the time when Alaska and Hawaii had entered the Union, at which point Heft's teacher changed the original grade to an "A." Heft has also copyrighted his designs for new American flags bearing 52 to 60 stars.

Carving a Legacy

He may have started out whittling a pair of pliers from a simple piece of wood as a young lad in the 1880s, but today Ernest "Mooney" Warther's more than 64 works of art are considered by the Smithsonian Institute as "priceless." Five generations later and the legacy left behind by Ernest and his wife Joan, along with the additions contributed by their children and grandchildren, are on display at the Warther's of Dover, a museum in the small city of Dover. The majority of Ernest's carvings chronicle the history of trains in wood, ivory and ebony. Not only are these miniature replicas carefully detailed, but they also come with moving parts—Ernest tailor-built the mechanisms required to create workable models. Added to the museum are the family's collection of arrowheads, hand-crafted knives and an assortment of button mosaic tiles created by Joan, an avid button collector since the age of 10. In fact, 73,282 of her more than 100,000 buttons are on display at the museum.

Words from Warther
"Start where you are and act as if no one is trying to hinder you."

World Claims

The city of Marion boasts several reasons to visit. It was the hometown of Warren G. Harding, the nation's 29th president; his previous residence has been turned into museum and his remains buried near the marble monument on site. Marion is home to the Wyandot Popcorn Museum and the city calls itself the "Popcorn Capital of the World." And if that's not enough, the stuffed carcass of Prince Imperial, the Percheron stallion that once belonged to Napoleon III of France in the 1800s, is also on display at the Marion County Historical Society Museum. It claims another world record as having the "World's Longest Mane."

Museum Oddities

From the outside, the Allen County Museum in Lima is quite stately looking, but venture inside and you'll be treated to some very odd displays indeed! Along with all the typical local artifacts most area museums have on display, this museum boasts a few extras—a room-sized replica of George Washington's plantation home in Mt. Vernon, a dead animal diorama of Noah's Ark, an iron lung, the jail cell where bank robber John Dillinger was housed after robbing the Citizen's National Bank of Bluffton of $2100 (complete with wax replicas of Dillinger and the sheriff, who was later killed by Dillinger's gang) and more.

The What Collection??

On the third floor of the Allen Memorial Medical Library of Case Western Reserve in Cleveland, there is a museum collection that is almost as old as sex itself. The Percy Skuy Collection on the History of Contraception showcases 650 items dating back as far as ancient Egypt and includes such curiosities as beaver testicle tea, a crocodile dung cup and the more recognizable birth control pill and intrauterine devices.

This unique collection was started 40 years ago by Mr. Skuy, a former president of the Canadian company Ortho Pharmaceutical. It began as a trade show novelty, but grew to become a unique historical example of social innovation and cultural politics.

Skuy, retired and living in Toronto, is still on the lookout for new items to add to his collection.

What's That You Said?

Here's another entry for the "weird museums" category. Tucked away in a corner of Kent State University is the Kenneth W. Berger Hearing Aid Museum and Archives. The museum outlines the history of the hearing aid and has more than 3000 different hearing aid models on display.

Oooh Baby!

In 1997, Belpre mayor Richard Thomas proclaimed his small community of about 6660 residents the "Baby Doll Capital of the World." Belpre is home to Lee Middleton Original Dolls, Inc. Established in 1978, the company considered one of the "nation's leading designer of collectible and play baby dolls." A seven-room, 2200 square foot museum containing antique and collectable dolls created by the company opened its doors in 2005.

Bed and Breakfast with a Twist

Sturgis House is a family-run bed and breakfast business in the Victorian-style mansion where, years earlier, another family-run business was housed. In the early years of the 20th century, E.G. Sturgis operated a funeral home out of his East Liverpool basement, and its claim to fame is that this was where the body of Charles Arthur "Pretty Boy" Floyd, public enemy number one back in 1934, was embalmed. Today, all that remains of the former mortuary is a collection of paraphernalia that includes the "death mask of Pretty Boy Floyd." It's said to hang over the washer and dryer, and the Dawson family who currently own the business will, if asked, give visitors a sneak peak.

Sad Memorial

Conquering the skies has always fascinated humankind, and among our first aircrafts was the dirigible—otherwise known as an airship. Eventually, it was replaced by modern aircraft, but in the early part of the 1900s, the dirigible was frequently used. Sadly, however, not all flights were successful, as the Airship Disaster Memorial in Ava can attest to. On the north side of town, on State Route 821, a monument commemorates the U.S.S. Shenandoah, which crashed there in 1925. It was the nation's first large dirigible to crash, killing 14 U.S. Navy air shipmen.

Cemented in History

Home improvement buffs likely know that George Bartholemew brought the "artificial stone" known as cement to the Midwest. The story goes that he convinced Bellefontaine's city council to pave a single street by guaranteeing the worthiness of cement as a material. And in 1891, Court Avenue became the nation's first concrete road. Today, signs boast it as the site of the "World's Oldest Concrete Street." Incidentally, Bellefontaine also claims another road-worthy world record. Apparently the entire 15 feet that makes up McKinley Street makes it the "World's Shortest Street."

Johnny Appleseed, Amen!

According to the Eastern Native Tree Society, the last surviving apple tree thought to be planted by Johnny Appleseed was discovered in 1994. Just how the Nova area farmer discovered the tree and attributed its existence to the gentle giant isn't clear... at least not to me. Other folks with Appleseed expertise dispute this, saying the last surviving tree he planted died in Jeromesville in 1965.

Prime Specimen
Since 1976, Brookville's Historical Society has opened Samuel Splinter's Queen Anne-style home to the public. Built in 1894, the home in its original splendor was saved from demolition through the efforts of the society and other community groups. Today, it serves as a museum with all the common artifacts—and a few odd ones besides. Tucked away in the basement is an exhibit of not one, but two rare animals. The stuffed head of

Andy D-Day, along with his taxidermic buddy the Two-Headed Calf, are on display for visitors to ogle at. In 1941, the Two-Headed Calf was born at the dairy farm owned by area residents Wilbur and Nessie Rasor. After the calf died, it was stuffed and the couple used it as a roadside attraction of sorts, charging folks a dime to catch a peek of the strange site. Andy D-Day came along a little later. He was an odd little bull born with four horns, four eyes and four nostrils in 1944. Recognizing another cash cow when they saw one, the Rasors purchased him in 1945, put him on display along side the Two-Headed Calf and upped the price of admission to a quarter. Andy D-Day died in 1956 and the Rasors had his head mounted and stuffed. The remains of both animals were donated to the Brookville Historical Society in 1976 and they, along with numerous photographs of the animals when they were alive, have been on display ever since.

Gahanna's proficiency in herb production started out back in the late 1800s, but it wasn't until 1972 when that community was officially recognized for it. That's when the government officially announced it as the "Herb Capital of Ohio."

Deep Dark Hole

If you can imagine, folks passing through Caldwell frequently detour to a small park at the junction of Highway 563 just to check out a hole in the ground. The story goes that two settlers, Silas Thorla and Robert McKee, discovered the first oil well in the entire continent in 1814 after noticing a deer licking the ground. They checked it out at first, thinking it might lead to the discovery of salt brine in the area, but instead they found oil. Apparently the men still drilled for salt brine and pumped it into barrels, only to find that the darned oil got in the way. Since the oil floated to the top of the salt brine, the men used wool blankets to soak it up. The entrepreneurial lot that they were, they then wrung out the blankets, collected the oil in bottles and began selling it as "Seneca Oil," a medicine said to cure everything from the common cold to rheumatism (I think I'd rather suffer through the disease!). In any case, the site is marked by a historic plaque dedicating the site as the Thorla-McKee Well. The well itself is still there, but it's surrounded by a metal-mesh cage. The state designated the site a "Great Ohio Adventure in Learning."

DID YOU KNOW?

The city of Steubenville was founded in 1797 and its history is chronicled in at least 25 different murals throughout the downtown and Hollywood Plaza areas. Among these memorials to the past is a mural of Dino Crocetti, more commonly known as Steubenville-born celebrity Dean Martin.

Everywhere a Sign

Cincinnati is home to the Cincinnati Reds, more than 80 glorious parks and the American Sign Museum. While it might not be the first on your list of things to do if you're passing through town, the American Sign Museum is well worth a visit. Tod Swormstedt, one-time publisher and editor of *Signs of the Times*, a magazine on the sign industry that's been around since 1906, came up with the idea. The media group that owned the magazine

agreed it was an interesting idea, financed some of the start-up
costs and in 1998 the American Sign Museum was born. There
are literally thousands of items on display, ranging from a full
fiberglass sculpture of the Frisch's Restaurant mascot Big Boy, to
neon signs, gold leaf signs, plastic signs and a photo collection
from the Douglas Leigh archives.

Praising the Passenger Pigeon

It is believed that the last passenger pigeon to grace the skies
died at the Cincinnati Zoo in 1914. Billions of passenger
pigeons blackened the skies at the time when Europeans began
arriving in North America. However, during the 19th century,
habitat loss and hunting decimated the population. By 1914, one
lone bird had survived. Named after Martha Washington, she
reportedly keeled over, falling from her perch at the ripe old age
of 29. To mark her demise, a bronze statue of Martha guards
the entrance to the pagoda aviary at the Cincinnati Zoo where
she lived. It's been named an official National Historic
Landmark. Martha's actual body, however, was frozen, shipped
to the Smithsonian Institute in Washington, D.C. and later
stuffed and added to its bird collection.

Odd Eatery

The 100th Bomb Group Restaurant, located across from the
Cleveland Hopkins International Airport, may seem like an
oddly-themed restaurant to those of us who aren't militarily
inclined. Inside, the restaurant's stucco walls are crowded with
pictures from the 100th Bomb Group and other World War II
memorabilia. Outside, makeshift minefields, checkpoints and
even a grounded fighter plane surround the eatery. But by all
accounts the food is great, even if the sounds of planes on take-
off and landing can make the experience seem a little too real.

Mobile TAM

Talk about seeing right through you. There are at least 17 gigantic, transparent women in the United States. These women were created a few decades ago as an educational tool for health museums. The first Transparent Anatomical Manikin (TAM), developed by designer Richard Rush in 1968, measured five feet, eight inches tall and revealed the inner workings of a woman— organs, muscles, skeleton, circulatory system and all. At the height of TAM-mania, Rush had produced 42. Of course, not all are in good repair today, but if you're in Cleveland, you can catch a glimpse of Juno, a 28-year-old replica of a woman, at HealthSpace on Euclid Avenue.

Take a Second Look

Creating sculptures from trees dates back to Roman times, but some of today's topiary gardens are likely very different from the originals. And if you're traveling down East Town Street in Columbus, you might want to check out one of the most original topiary parks around. Designer James T. Mason built the metal frames for the park in 1989 and it must have been some feat too. Altogether there are 54 people, eight boats, three dogs, a monkey and a cat: and together they form a life-sized recreation of a painting by Georges Seurat entitled, *A Sunday Afternoon on the Isle of La Grand Jatte.*

Labor of Love

Back in the Dirty Thirties, Springfield resident H.G. "Ben" Hartman found himself with a whole lot of energy and no paid labor to put it to good use on. So he got busy building. At first, he collected stone and bits of mirror, pottery and other found objects in the hope of building a fish pond in his backyard. But once it was completed and he went on to build stone houses, churches, castles and even a replica of Philadelphia's Independence Hall and the White House, it was clear he'd caught the "dementia concretia" bug. Who knew an obsessive compulsive drive to grab whatever objects one can find and use them for continuously building had a name? Either way, the end result is a completely transformed backyard that's attracted visitors since the last of the estimated quarter of a million stones was laid in 1939. At the time of this book's publication folks passing by 1905 Russell Avenue could still check it out for themselves. Ben Junior inherited the house from his father and has attempted to keep their family's backyard creations in good order. Still, he is hoping to sell the property to someone who will maintain the site, so before you make a special trip you might want to Google Hartman's Rock Garden and check out its status.

Bigger and Better?

It measures 405 feet and 10 inches in length, is lined with more than 100 stools and 56 beer taps and rose from the ashes of the Colonial, an historic hotel burned in a 1988 fire. Located in Put-in-Bay, the Beer Barrel Saloon has a seating capacity of 1200—not bad for a town with a population of 128, according to the 2000 Census.

Monument to a Pig

Back in the 1850s, the Shaker community had a market monopoly on hogs. They had the biggest, the fastest-growing and the best-selling hogs in the state, an exclusive breed called the Big China. However, the Shakers were a celibate bunch and began to die out for obvious reasons. A local farmer, a Polish immigrant by the name of Asher Asher, sensed opportunity and managed to buy two of the Shaker's best sows and one of their boars. Soon, Asher's new breed of pigs began outselling any other on the market. By the 1860s, this type of hog had spread across the country and folks in the pig-breeding business thought it needed a name and class of its own. After tracing its ancestry, they decided to name the hog breed the Poland China hog and commemorate the occasion by erecting a monument of the popular animal. Quite possibly the first pig statue in America, it can still be seen at the intersection of Towne Boulevard and State Route 25 in Blue Ball.

Concrete Corn

There are 109 concrete corn cobs standing erect at the Sam and Eulalia Frantz Park in Dublin. Sculptor and university professor Malcolm Cochran was commissioned to create the work in 1994 to commemorate the agricultural heritage of the area in general and the work of Sam and Eulalia Frantz in particular. The site was once the Frantz family farm, and Sam was a leading corn hybridizer in the mid 20th century.

Calling All Visitors!

Although Canal Winchester is a relatively small community, with a population just under 4500 according to the 2000 Census, there's certainly no shortage of interesting sites for visitors to check out. Along with the assortment of antique shops and historic sites maintained by the local historical society, the town is home to the Mid-Ohio Doll and Toy Museum (which features thousands of dolls among its displays of antique toys), the Barbers Museum and Hall of Fame (and its collection of more than 50 barber poles and assorted paraphernalia) and the Slate Run Vineyard (which hosts open houses at various times throughout the year).

DID YOU KNOW?

The American Whistle Corporation of Columbus has been manufacturing whistles since 1956. It's the only plant of its kind in the country.

YOU'VE GOTTA SEE THIS—MUST-SEE PLACES

The Evolution of a Museum

The Wood County Historical Museum in Bowling Green had a rather unorthodox beginning. Initially, the simple structure built in 1865 on 160 acres of land was called a "poor farm"— a publicly run housing operation for the poor, needy and sometimes infirm. On February 15, 1971, the remaining residents, most of whom were elderly nursing home patients, were moved to another location and the county commissioners of the day suggested tearing down the site. That's when Lyle Fletcher and the Wood County Historical Society got on board, lobbying for the building to be transformed into a museum. They were successful, and in 1975, the Wood County Historical Museum opened to the public with just three rooms' worth of exhibits. Among these are "three human fingers in a jar," formerly attached to a murdered Mary Bach, the knife used to cut off the fingers and the noose used to hang the perpetrator of the dastardly deed. Today, most of the building has been transformed to accommodate historical exhibits from the area, but the finger display, which can be found in the Government Room, continues to draw folks attracted by the macabre.

Holy Relics

Folks into religious history will be amazed by the Shrine of the Holy Relics in Maria Stein. The shrine began when Father J. Gartner gave a collection of relics he'd been given in Rome to the Sisters of the Precious Blood in 1875. A chapel was constructed and the Maria Stein Centre born. Throughout the chapel slivers of bones once belonging to Catholic saints hang;

items thought to have once belonged to Jesus are on display, and the body of Saint Victoria was put to rest under the Sacred Heart Altar. Well over 100 saints are represented at the chapel.

Double-Take

Yes, that is a real castle you see. Folks traveling through Loveland may not believe their eyes, but back in 1929 an ambitious Sunday school teacher and local newspaper man named Harry Andrews acquired a piece of land along the Little Miami River. He dedicated an hour or so a week, whatever he could spare from his other duties, and started building a life-sized replica of a British castle of the Roman era. The initial idea was to build a castle where his Boy Scout troop, the "Knights of the Golden Trail," would be able to play and fish and have parties. Of course it took much longer than he thought to complete his ambitious project—he continued building until his death and is said to have created the "safest bomb shelter in the entire state of Ohio" in his castle's dungeon. With the exception of the ballroom, which is one-fifth the full size, everything was built to scale. At Andrews' death in 1981, the castle was willed to the now adult-version of the Knights of the Golden Trail. They continue to maintain the site, open it up for visitors and rent it out for special events. And if you decide to make an overnight of it, beware. There have been several reports of haunted happenings!

Three-Dimensional Bible

It's yet another museum with a twist. The Living Bible Museum, located in Mansfield, takes visitors through a tour of biblical history with wax sculptures set in full-scale scenes. More than 70 scenes tell the stories of King Solomon, Noah and the Ark, the Last Supper, the Annunciation and more. The idea for creating this museum came about after Pastor Richard Diamond and his wife Alwilda visited a wax museum in Atlanta, Georgia, in the 1970s. The story goes that the couple were surprised and moved to tears when they came to the final display, a scene of Jesus' Ascension. They reasoned that a museum filled with such scenes would bring the Bible to life for everyone who visited. The idea didn't come to a reality until the end of 1983, when three scenes were unveiled. Initially they were on display at the Diamond Hill Cathedral, but soon the pastor and his followers felt called to build a museum on church property, and by 1986 a building had been erected and six scenes prepared for viewing. It was officially opened to the public on August 15, 1987.

Looking to the Skies

Aviation enthusiasts in the neighborhood of Dayton should consider taking in the National Museum of the United States Air Force. What began with a display of a few World War I fighter planes and assorted paraphernalia in the corner of a downtown aircraft hanger back in 1923 has developed into a full-fledged museum located at Wright-Patterson Air Force Base. Today, the museum includes more than 300 aircraft and missiles, plus thousands of aviation artifacts.

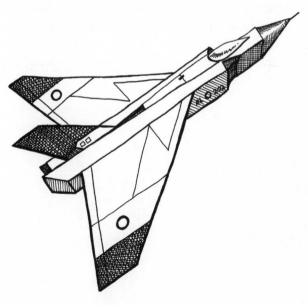

Mr. President, Sir!

Hartsgrove boasts another one-of-a-kind when it comes to museums. Nick Pahys Jr., DDG-CH-AdVS-A.G.E.-LDA-FIBA and Ambassador of Grand Eminence, (and if you understand what all these letters mean I certainly applaud you!), founded the Presidential Museum in Hartsgrove back in 1992 after decades of research that forms a reeducation, of sorts, for everyone in the nation. You see, Pahys argues, very convincingly I might add, that George Washington was not the country's first president but that, in fact, John Hanson was. George Washington didn't come along until nine years and seven additional presidents later! Pahys explains that Hanson became the country's first president in 1781 under the Articles of Confederation, also referred to as our nation's "first constitution." George Washington didn't take the title of first American president until 1789, under the "Second Federal Constitution." Still, it appalled Pahys that one of America's founding fathers was so forgotten that he wasn't even "mentioned in encyclopedias until 1929 and that only one book has been published about his life." Although his museum features "all 51 presidents," John Hanson plays a prominent role.

National Imperial Glass Museum

If grandma's cupboards contain a bowl, goblet or any other glass item created by the Imperial Glass, you might want to take a trip to the nearest *Antiques Roadshow* and have it appraised. The company organized in Bellaire in 1901, but it wasn't until 1904 when its first glass products were produced. At the time there were so many glass factories in Bellaire that it was nicknamed the Glass City and the newbie on the block just added to its reputation. The 80-year history of the plant, along with samples from of their product, is chronicled in the National Imperial Glass Museum, located at 3200 Belmont Street.

Saluting Hopalong

Fans of the film and television Hopalong Cassidy classics likely know there were more than 100 episodes made starring William Boyd. Saluting the golden age of the character that Boyd created is the Hopalong Cassidy Museum in Cambridge. Created by Laura Bates, the museum is packed with photographs, posters, full-size Hopalong mannequins and all manner of assorted paraphernalia.

Limestone Caverns

Located just outside of Delaware, about 20 minutes north of Route 40 is an underground world like no other. Known as the Olentangy Indian Caverns, this labyrinth of underground limestone caves was believed to be formed by a powerful underground river. While the first white man to discover the caves is believed to have been J.M. Adams in 1821, the Wyandot Indians were believed to have inhabited the caves long before that. Visitors to the site descend into the three levels of the cavern by a concrete stairway to a depth of 105 feet, but that's just as far as the site has been developed to date. Some exploration has continued to a fourth level where an underground river is flowing to the Olentangy River. Outside the cave entrance the site has been further developed to include other amenities such as a miniature western village, an 18-hole miniature golf course and a climbing wall.

Yes, It's Spelled Correctly

Another museum with a twist...or have I said that before? Ohio seems to be filled with them. In any case, The Blair Museum of Lithophanes in Toledo salutes the lithophane—a porcelain artpiece that, when backlit, exposes a beautiful image. The unique artwork was quite popular during the 1800s in Europe and is often as useful as it is pleasing to the eye. Lithophanes are often shaped and used as lampshades, fire screens, sun catchers and such. With more than 2300 antique lithophanes on display, the museum claims to have "the largest collection of these unique porcelain pictures in the world." While founder Laurel Blair often opened his home to share his collection with those interested, the museum was formed after his death in 1993 when he bequeathed his collection "to the people of the city of Toledo." The museum is currently housed in the Toledo Botanical Garden on Elmer Drive.

Saluting the Bicycle

Built for one or two, the Bicycle Museum of America in New Bremen likely has a sample or two from every era for you to observe. For a relatively small community with a population of less than 3000, according to 2002 data, the museum boasts an impressive 1000 bikes in its collection, displaying 300 at any given time. That means repeat visits usually uncover some new treasure to examine. And if you can't make it into town, check out the museum's website for a virtual tour.

RECORD BREAKERS AND FIRSTS

☛ While ancient Greeks were believed to have created a type of chewing gum from tree resin, historians credit Ohioan Amos Tyler with being the first to patent the stuff often stuck to the bottom of a table on July 27, 1869.

☛ Flying and all things aeronautic were thought a man's purview, but Lauretta Schimmoler was the first American woman to challenge that way of thinking back in 1929. That's when she started managing the Bucyrus airfield and became the first woman in the U.S. to run an airport.

☛ The first woman credited with flying around the world solo was Jerrie Mock of Columbus. Her historic 29-day trip took place in 1964.

☛ The first college in the U.S. to admit women was Oberlin College in Oberlin, Ohio. The year: 1833.

☛ Ohioans like to claim America's first traffic light was erected in Cleveland on August 5, 1914, but that has been challenged. Folks in Utah believe the first one was actually erected in their city two years earlier.

☛ The Cincinnati Reds (then known as the Cincinnati Red Stockings) became the world's first professional baseball team by using baseball as a promotional gimmick. The idea was the brainchild of attorney Aaron B. Chapman, and the team's inaugural year was 1869.

☛ The American Federation of Labor (AFL), one of the nation's first labor unions, was founded by Samuel Gompers in Columbus in 1886. The group joined with the Congress of Industrial Organizations (CIO) in 1935, and today the

AFL-CIO is considered the country's dominant labor organization.

☞ The city of Fostoria bridges three counties: Seneca, Hancock and Wood. It's believed to be the only city to do so.

☞ Sources differ as to dates and times, but the general consensus credits John Lambert of Ohio City as having made the country's first automobile, way back in 1891.

☞ The history books credit Charles Goodyear of Akron as having discovered how to vulcanize rubber in 1839. Goodyear patented his idea in 1844 and went on to create an empire based on the product, but evidence suggests that balls and other rubberized objects existed as far back as 1600 BC.

☞ New Carlisle-born Roy J. Plunkett was a chemist who was said to have "accidentally" invented Teflon back in 1938. In 1973, he was inducted into the Plastics Hall of Fame, and in 1985 into the Inventors Hall of Fame for his invention of Teflon and other DuPont products.

☞ The first African American to be elected to public office was John Mercer Langston when he took on the position of town clerk of Brownhelm Township in 1855.

☞ The first African American to win an Olympic Gold medal was William DeHart Hubbard. The year was 1924 and the event was the running long jump.

☞ You can't blame clumsy footwork for not wanting to jump rope any longer. In February of 2006, U.S. patent #7037243 was issued for the Cordless Jump Rope. Lester Clancy of Mansfield devised two handles with moving ball bearings inside. Their movement gives users the feel of a rope twirling without the problems incurred by getting their feet all tied up!

- Attention all news-hounds. If you're tied to the 24-hour cable news channel CNN, listen up! Cincinnati proudly claims CNN founder Robert (Ted) Turner as one of its own.

- The Kroger Co. is the top grocery retailer in the U.S. and owes its success to its innovative founder Bernard Henry Kroger. Kroger sunk his life savings into the idea of opening a grocery store with a twist in Cincinnati in 1883. It was the first grocery store to also house a meat market and bakery.

- Students at Ohio State University in Columbus broke an international speed record when they built the Buckeye Bullet in 2004. The electric car clocked 271 miles per hour, making it the "World's Fastest Electric Car."

- The sunny day favorite, the Good Humor Bar, first appeared in Youngstown. That's because in 1920 a local candy maker there named Harry Burt created the ice cream treat.

- You can't miss the world's oldest barefoot water skier, George Blair. Also known as "Banana George" because of his flashy yellow wetsuit, Blair trick-skied barefoot in Cypress Gardens, Florida, on February 20, 2005. The Toledo-born Blair was 90 years old at the time.

- This "first" was at one time heralded as the "World's Number One Fun Car" and the "World's Most Exciting Small Car." The King Midget Car, a compact, single-cylinder vehicle created by Claud Dry and Dale Orcutt in 1946, was manufactured by the Midget Motors Corporation until 1970. It must have been a hit for quite a few people because, for several years during that time, it was named the "6th largest automobile manufacturer" in the country.

☞ The Columbus Zoo went down in history as home to the first baby gorilla born in captivity. Baby Columbus (or Colo for short) was born in 1956.

☞ The first automatic glass-blowing machine was invented by Toledo resident Michael Joseph Owens in 1903.

☞ The first automatic drip coffee maker was invented by Cleveland resident Vincent Marotta in 1972. With a keen understanding of the power of personality in advertising, Marotta acquired baseball superstar Joe DiMaggio to promote the product.

☞ Before Play-Doh was a playtime staple, it was nothing more than wallpaper cleaner. In 1956, Joseph McVicker, owner of Kutol Products of Cincinnati, decided to scent the product and marketed it as a toy. At first, Play-Doh was a dullish gray, but the next year McVicker added color.

☞ In 1920, Cleveland celebrated a baseball first when Indians' pitcher Jim Bagby made history as the "first pitcher to hit a home run in a World Series game."

☞ The state's first radio station hit the airwaves in 1947. Cleveland's WEWS-TV was also credited with broadcasting the "first live remote of a Cleveland Indians baseball game" the following year.

☞ The mentoring organizations Big Brother and Big Sister have their roots in Cincinnati. Back in 1903, businessman Irvin Westheimer fed and befriended a hungry and lonely boy. The experience was so rewarding he encouraged his friends to do the same and the rest, as they say, is history.

☞ The first African American to play major league baseball was Moses Fleetwood Walker. He was 27 when he signed with the Toledo Blue Stockings in 1883.

☛ The country's first Medal of Honor was awarded to Private Jacob Parrot on March 25, 1863 for his role in sabotaging "Confederate railroads during the Civil War."

☛ Here she comes…Columbus' Mary Campbell was the only person to earn herself the title of Miss America twice, in 1922 and 1923. That was before new rules restricted contestants to one competition.

FOOD AND FESTIVALS

Food—Contributing to the Girth of a Nation

It's true—you'll never go hungry in Ohio. The state is home base to four fast food chains and several sit-down restaurants: Wendy's, White Castle, Charley's Grilled Subs, Steak Escape, Bob Evans Restaurants, Max & Erma's, Damon's Grill and Donato's Pizza.

Ohio is also home to a heaping helping of culinary innovations such as:

- ☛ Girl Scout Cookies—in 1930 Girl Scouts in Akron asked the Albrecht Grocery Company to make 100,000 of their cookies, the first Girl Scouts in the U.S. to employ a commercial baker. Within four years, all of the nation's Girl Scout cookies were bakery-made.

- ☛ Ripple potato chips—Emerson Cain of Bowling Green laid claim to the first wavy potato chips. He called them "marcelle" because they resembled a popular hairdo in the 1930s.

- ☛ Breakfast cereal—Ferdinand Schumacher sold his oatmeal to hungry Union soldiers. His ground grains were cheap, tasty and cooked quickly. They were a big hit with the soldiers and the demand for his cereal led the way for Schumacher's mills to become the Quaker Oats Company.

- ☛ Cincinnati Chili—Macedonian immigrant Athanas Kiradjieff invented what we now call "Cincinnati Chili," the unofficial food of the city by the same name. Cincinnati chili is markedly different from regular chili: it is thinner than its traditional Texas counterpart and is made with a variety of exotic ingredients, such as cinnamon, chocolate, allspice and Worcestershire sauce. The result is a subtly sweet, slightly spicy, faintly smoky chili that is unlike any other. It is usually served over pasta and is topped with cheese, onions and sometimes beans, but it is always served with oyster crackers.

☛ Johnny Marzetti—Mary Marzetti of the Marzetti Restaurant created her now famous beef, cheese and tomato casserole back in the 1900s and named it for her husband.

☛ Life Savers—Clevelander Clarence Crane was a chocolate maker by trade but decided to think out of the box by experimenting with a round peppermint candy. He punched holes in the middle of them and advertised the candy as useful "for that stormy breath."

☛ The hot dog—Niles native Harry M. Stevens is credited for the idea of combining a bun and its dog; a New York newspaper caricature of the frankfurter originated the name "hot dog."

Festivals—Always a Reason to Party!

It appears that Avon has declared itself the "Duct Tape Capital of the World"—and it hosts an annual festival to prove it! Since June 2003, the town has hosted the Avon Heritage Duct Tape Festival on Father's Day weekend. The salute to the sticky wonder doesn't end with the name. Oh no! Duct tape is front and centre at all times, with entertainment provided by The Duct Tape Guys, a live Duct Tape Fashion Show and even the announcement of a Duct Tape Dad of the Year. So if you're tired of plain, old-fashioned, apple-pie-and-ice-cream fairs, plan to check this festival out. It promises to be a one-of-a-kind experience.

A Big Fish Story

If you're into fishing, chances are you've been to a fishing festivity of some type. To add to your repertoire of tall tales, the next time you're in Port Clinton on New Year's Eve check out Walleye Madness at Midnight. For the last 12 years townsfolk and visitors alike have gathered in the downtown area on New Year's Eve and watched as a 20-foot long, 600-pound walleye named Captain Wylie was lowered to the ground at the stroke of midnight. Everything you ever wanted to know about the event can be found on its website (just Google the festival's name), including a countdown to the next time when Captain Wylie will be lowered from his perch atop of one of Port Clinton's downtown buildings in days, hours, minutes and seconds.

Celebrating the Crooner

Every year since 1996, the year following his death, the city of Steubenville has celebrated the accomplishments of their favorite son, Dean Martin. The festival, which is usually held over the Father's Day weekend, highlights the man and his music with Dean Martin Singing Contests, tributes, live shows and a Father's Day buffet. Dean Martin was born in Steubenville in 1917 and died on Christmas Day, 1995.

Gourd Mania

Since 1963, gourds have been the focus of festival activities in Mount Gilead. At one time the town hosted what was considered the "World's Largest Gourd Festival," but in 2006 the show was moved to the Drake County Fairgrounds in Greenville. Still, if you've a hankering for the ornamental crop, you might want to consider checking it out. The event is usually held in September or October.

A Bit of the Emerald Isle

In a community with a name like Dublin, it makes sense for the annual festival to have an Irish theme. Since 1987, the Dublin Irish Festival boasts traditional music, dance, food, crafts, medieval demonstrations, costumes and so much more. It's held each year in early August.

Bratwurst Bonanza

Bucyrus owes a hefty portion of its heritage to butchers who immigrated to the fair city from Germany. After settling in Ohio, immigrant butchers perfected the food known as the bratwurst—a sausage made from pork and beef. The butchers' reputations for this fine food grew so much that Bucyrus is now known as the "Bratwurst Capital of America." The city celebrates its specialty every year in mid-August, often attracting 100,000 visitors annually.

Popcorn Party

With over a quarter of a million visitors each year, the Marion Popcorn Festival is the biggest celebration of its kind in the world. Conceived by three businessmen as a way of promoting the city as well as its largest production crop, the Marion Popcorn Festival has grown to become a top-billed family attraction that lasts for three days in early September.

Sweet Corn Festival

The sleepy town of Millersport transforms each year into a bustling center of food, fun and country music during the week leading up to Labor Day. Showcasing Grande Ole Opry legends and current country music entertainers, the festival celebrates the traditional end of the growing season for corn. If you like good, old-fashioned country food paired with good entertainment, then this festival is a must-see.

The Circleville Pumpkin Show

This event is unique in that it is the oldest festival in the state of Ohio. It is the sixth largest festival in the United States, with annual attendance in the 300,000 mark, and it bills itself as the "The Greatest Free Show on Earth" because there is no admission charge. It started with humble origins in 1903 as an agricultural exhibit and small street fair and has grown into a remarkable and fascinating community affair. The festival is usually held in October.

A Salute to the Tomato

While many people in the early days of the U.S. grew tomatoes as ornamental plants, not many enjoyed the fruits as an edible treat. It would take the persistence of a man named Alexander Livingston to cultivate many of the varieties of tomatoes enjoyed today. Residing and working in Reynoldsburg as a seed and plant horticulturalist, Livingston's goal was to create a fruit that was tastier, smoother and more reliable than the wild tomatoes that were available. After years of experimenting, he introduced the tomato plant known as the Paragon in 1870. Able to be easily grown and commercially processed without loss of flavor or quality, the Paragon tomato became a superstar in the crop world and is now grown in every state in the nation.

Reynoldsburg pays tribute to Livingston's innovation each year by holding the Tomato Festival the first week in September. Tomato exhibits and contests, as well as free tomato juice are the highlights of this botanical fruit festival.

HAUNTINGS

Creepy Ohio

Just about every source on reported hauntings in Ohio agree about one thing—you're never far away from yet another ghostly tale. Sightings, eerie encounters, weird happenings, poltergeists, just about any type of ghost-related apparition have a story told about them in this state.

☛ Stoking the family furnace with coal seems to have led to the demise of one Athens-area resident. Apparently her furnace exploded and since then her endless screams have plagued Screaming Hollow, the name given to the area near Luhrig Road.

☞ There are about 2000 former patients of the Athens State Hospital buried in graveyards surrounding the site. Sadly, most grave markers don't provide the names of the deceased. They just stand there, a ghostly presence. And then, of course, there are the ghosts who appear from time to time and, after all, can you blame them?

☞ If she's any good it's hard to imagine complaining about the ghost of the violin-playing woman who wanders the hall-ways of Carroll County's Cox Mansion. Of course, the cry-ing baby, angry suicide victim and headless horseman could be a little more difficult to ignore.

☞ The Route 513 Bridge in Guernsey County's Quaker City, according to some legends, seems to have a ghostly carriage rider who likes to tap pedestrians on the shoulder.

☞ Sad stories make for unhappy spirits. Such is the case of Urbana's Hell House. After a distraught husband and father lost his family in a train accident, he completed the home he was supposed to live in with his family, then committed suicide. His spirit is believed to still linger there.

☞ This one almost appears to make sense, where ghosts are concerned. Apparently folks passing by Lake County's Fairport Harbor Lighthouse had reported hearing the meow of a ghostly feline. It's not certain if the discovery of its mummified remains, which were removed from a crawl-space, rectified the situation or not.

☞ Folks passing along Medina County's I-71 have reported seeing a male hitchhiker in a tan coat that, by all accounts, becomes transparent as the car approaches.

☞ Jails aren't very nice places—especially ones that house a
Death Row section. Over the Easter weekend of 1993, a riot
at the Lucasville penitentiary in Scioto County certainly
looked to cement that idea. More than 20 people died in
that bloody confrontation, and today guards and prisoners
alike report seeing shadows, hearing doors slam and other
unexplained mysteries.

GHOST TOWNS

Nice Places to Visit, But You Wouldn't Want to Live There

Since Ohio was opened up to white settlement in 1787, after investors purchased 1.5 million acres for potential development, it's no surprise that the state has an interesting selection of ghost towns. Some are just shells of what they once were. Others may have a handful or so of assorted residents hanging on to the hope that new life will be breathed into their beloved community. Here are just a few interesting sites to consider visiting, should you be in their neck of the woods:

Building Utopia

The sad story of Utopia began back in 1844, when a group of Fouriers (followers of a French sect that believed if they shut themselves off from the rest of the world, they could create their own Utopian society), founded a community in Clermont County near the Ohio River. Despite their beliefs and dedication, this utopia was relatively short-lived. On December 13, 1847, Ohio experienced one of the biggest floods of the 19th century. That day the remaining followers of the fledgling community, which was sold in 1846 to John O. Wattles, the leader of yet another sect, were celebrating in the town hall. Against the advice of area residents, Wattles had moved the hall to the nearby Ohio River and, you guessed it, the banks overflowed and almost everyone was swept away and died. Of course the population of the town, which was already severely depleted of residents, dwindled further. Today all that remains are a few families, a general store, an Ohio Historical Marker memorializing Utopia for all time and the many ghosts said to haunt the banks of the Ohio River on rainy nights.

Tales of Terror!

The ghost town of Knockemstiff claims several ghostly encounters and unusual experiences. Folks reported strange sightings at the old cemetery near Donald's Pond, in the 1700s. Devil's Leap is said to be haunted by the spirit of a fellow who jumped to his death because he said he was "haunted by the voice of the devil in his head." One strange story tells of a man lounging across a stretch of road called Foggymoore (because of the fog that constantly collects there), his hand in one hand and a cigarette in another. Apparently when a car happened along he just "floated away." And another story tells of how the body of a beauty named Lindy Sue was discovered on the Paint Creek Bridge—strangled after she was thought to be meeting with her boyfriend. He was never heard from again, nor was his body ever found. But Lindy Sue, by all accounts, is still there—folks have heard her howling.

A Sort of Ghost Town

Perry County is home to a village named Shawnee. While 2000 Census figures reported 608 people still lived in Shawnee, its population has depleted to such an extent that it's been considered a "semi ghost town" of sorts. Founded in 1873 to provide home for the area's coal miners, the community at one point swelled to a population of more than 7000. Today, many of Shawnee's original buildings have been torn down or boarded up, but tour what remains, check out archival photos and you can't help but feel you've traveled back in time.

Unsettled Spirits

San Toy is another Perry County company town formed around the coal-mining industry before 1900. While little evidence, structurally speaking, remains of San Toy, legends still reverberate. One story goes that although mine owners were good to their employees, in between shifts workers had little to do but drink their time away. Add firearms to the mix, which most men carried with them, and it was said there was a murder a day. If that's even partially true, it must make for at least a few unsettled spirits hanging about.

The Lights Have Gone Out on This Town
In the spring of 2002, the United States Environmental Protection Agency put American Electric Power, which operated a coal-fueled power plant directly on Cheshire's town's outskirts, on alert because the toxic plumes of sulfurous gas spewing from the plant were poisoning the air, making residents ill. The EPA required so many operational adjustments to make the area safe for residents that it was less expensive for the AEP to buy everyone out instead. A few folks chose to remain, but for the most part, today Cheshire is little more than a ghost town. At the time this book was printed, the plant continues to produce the clouds of gas that contributed to the demise of this little Ohio town.

Disappeared

A modern apartment building in the Cleveland neighborhood of Collingwood, with the Carlisle Cemetery occupying a portion of its courtyard, is all that remains of a community named Hibernia. Hibernia was a very small blip on the map; fewer than a handful of families lived there. But from 1849 to 1857 it did have its own post office and until the 1940s the bus stopped in town. All the houses that were once there are gone, but a sign outside the apartment complex, Hibernia Apartment Homes, aptly echoes the town's previous name.

OVERSIZED CLAIMS

Big Things and Strange Structures

Here are a few that claim to be the world's largest—or at the very least, very big.

☛ Berlin claims to have the World's Largest Amish Buggy. It apparently is more than 10 feet tall, 13 feet and 9 inches wide and weighs about 1200 pounds. You can check it out for yourself at the Wendell August Forge.

☛ The World's Largest Cuckoo Clock apparently lives in Wilmot. It measures 23 feet high, 24 feet wide and 13 feet, 6 inches deep, and like any other cuckoo clock, its figurines come to life on the hour. You can visit the clock at the Grandma's Alpine Homestead Restaurant and Clock Shop.

☛ At one time Big Muskie was considered the "World's Largest Earth Moving Machine," but its status in that arena has been undoubtedly replaced since it was built in 1969. What remains of the 13,500-ton piece of machinery is little more than the bucket used to scoop and move "39 million pounds of earth and rock every hour," but folks can check it out, along with a detailed description of its history and vital statistics, at Reinersville's Miner's Memorial Park.

☛ Windsor boasts the "World's Largest Virgin Mary Statue." Located on an area farm at 6569 Ireland Road, the statue was erected by residents Ed and Pat Heinz. Between the image of Mary and the angel and cloud that forms her base, the sculpture tops the 50-foot mark. It was officially dedicated on August 5, 1995. Since then another Virgin Mary statue built in the Balkans claims to be the world's largest.

☛ Fact or fiction? Depending on your resourcefulness and abilities of detection, you may or may not uncover the World's Largest Loaf of Bread, which according to roadside travelers who chronicle their tales on the Internet, is mighty hard to find. Apparently it's located at the American Pan manufacturing company in Urbana, but not many know of its existence.

☛ Anyone looking for the nation's only washboard manufacturer can't miss the building when they see it. The Columbus Washboard Company in Logan advertises its presence with the World's Largest Washboard attached to the side of its building. It was built sometime after 1999, is constructed of wood and metal and is 24 feet tall.

☛ A roadside marker once called attention to a giant footprint-like impression on a section of rock near an old gas station outside of Orangeburg on Route 40, on the north side of the road, 1.6 miles west of State Route 726. The footprint has generated great controversy over the years, some saying that the impression is that of the devil. Apparently the roadside marker has gone missing, but the impression is still there, if you care to search for it.

☞ Paul Bunyan must have made a big impression on the American public, since there are dozens of giant Paul Bunyan statues dotting the countryside. Ohio's salute to the timber-master, a 17 foot replica, is located at Hocking College.

☞ Well-known author and humorist Erma Bombeck's final resting place is marked in a rather unusual way. Buried at the Woodland Cemetery in Dayton, a 29,000-pound rock was hauled all the way from her home in Arizona to her grave and was placed on her plot to commemorate her years living in the Southwest.

☞ At a height of 352 feet, Perry's Victory and International Peace Memorial is the third-tallest memorial in the country. Construction on the monument, which was erected in honor of Commodore Oliver Hazard Perry for his efforts in the War of 1812, began in 1912, and it was ready for public viewing in 1915.

DISASTROUS EVENTS

Twister Terror

In 1974, the town of Xenia became ground zero for the nation's worst tornado. This super storm spawned 148 tornadoes in 13 states and one Canadian province, but the monster tornado that formed outside the town of Xenia on that fateful day of April 4 would cause the most deaths.

Registering as an F5 on the Fujita Scale, the most intense rating, this tornado formed no less than six separate funnels within itself as it entered the city limits. As wide as half a mile, it laid waste to everything in its path, including 300 homes, 9 churches and 7 of the city's 9 schools; it damaged half the remaining buildings in this town of 27,000, leaving 34 people dead. As it left town, it blew a nearby traveling train off its tracks and then deposited three semi-tractor trucks on the roof of the bowling alley. It would take Xenia several months to recover and in the process of rebuilding, the town installed tornado sirens and built a memorial for the victims.

The Silver Bridge Tragedy

On December 15, 1967, the U.S. Highway 35 Bridge that connected Ohio and West Virginia at the towns of Kanauga and Point Pleasant suddenly collapsed, taking with it the lives of 46 people.

The bridge was built in 1928 and was dubbed the Silver Bridge because of its aluminum paint, the first of its kind in the country. Constructed by the General Corporation and the American Bridge Company, the bridge featured innovative designs such as high-tension eye-bar chains and rocker towers, which allowed the bridge to flex with shifting loads and temperature-induced chain length variations. This type of suspension bridge had been in use for about 100 years without incident.

Constructed at a time when Model T Fords were the standard in driving, the bridge began experiencing greater loads as cars became heavier and traffic became a constant. In 1967, the Silver Bridge was holding loads triple the amount it was designed for. As a result, a small crack formed, measuring only one-tenth of an inch and undetectable by either human eye or that day's current technology. In the cold of that afternoon, the crack gave way and the bridge collapsed, plunging into the dark waters of the Ohio River. The collapse of the Silver Bridge sent a shock wave though the nation, causing President Lyndon B. Johnson to order a nation-wide safety probe of bridges.

A new bridge was built in 1969 and was named the Silver Memorial Bridge.

A flurry of paranormal activity and bizarre sightings plagued the Kanauga and Point Pleasant areas up to the day of the Silver Bridge collapse. Many people believe the two were somehow related and the popular theory was dramatized in the 2002 Richard Gere movie called *The Mothman Prophecies*. Point Pleasant even has a yearly event called the Mothman Festival to celebrate the folklore and mystery surrounding this truly weird happening.

A BRIEF HISTORY OF OHIO

"Leave the land east of the Alleghenies for the use of Indians..."
—King George III, in his 1763 proclamation to his American subjects, telling them to leave the Ohio territory alone

Natives Had First Dibs

What is now Ohio first belonged to several indigenous tribes. Native Americans had inhabited the area for several thousand years, but by 1600, the majority of its residents had become victims of either disease or war. By the 1700s, the land west and north of the Ohio River became the territory of the powerful New York state-based Iroquois nation and home to the refugee remnants of East Coast tribes and other devastated Native groups.

Trading Game

It is widely accepted that the first white man to see the land now called Ohio was René Robert Cavalier, sieur de La Salle. France turned the territory over to Britain in 1763 after losing the French and Indian Wars. The British had no ambition to colonize it. They simply wanted the land for its established— and very lucrative—fur trade. All that changed with the American Revolution, and by 1783, the lands were ceded to the United States.

Immediately, New York, Connecticut and Virginia expressed interest in the resource-rich land. A group of American Revolutionary War veterans formed a group called the Ohio Company of Virginia, a land speculation company formed to colonize Ohio, but final boundary placements were arranged with The Northwest Ordinance of 1787, which also included the decree that slavery was illegal. Connecticut and Virginia reserved the right to use part of the Ohio territory as payment to Revolutionary War veterans. The reserved land went by the names of the Connecticut Western Reserve and the Virginia Military District.

DID YOU  KNOW?

Marietta, Ohio's first city, was founded by a group known as the Ohio Company (also known as the Ohio Company of Associates). The name Marietta came from Marie Antoinette, the Queen of France, who had helped the American colonies in their fight with Britain.

Ohio Becomes Official…Twice

On February 19, 1803, President Jefferson approved Ohio's boundaries and constitution. However, the current custom of Congress declaring an official date of statehood didn't begin until 1812. In 1953, President Eisenhower signed a retroactive act that officially declared March 1, 1803 as the date of Ohio's admittance into the Union.

EARLY LEADERS

Anthony Wayne (1745–96)

General Anthony Wayne (known as "Mad Anthony" because of his vigorously noisy battlefield performances) was given the job of getting rid of the Indian threat in the Ohio Territory in 1793. General Wayne marched his army north from around the Cincinnati area, establishing forts along the way, including Fort Greene Ville. His army met up with the Native American forces in what is now Maumee at a place where several trees lay on the ground, uprooted by a tornado. General Wayne's army soundly defeated the Indians and the Battle of Fallen Timbers, as it is now called, led to the signing of the Greenville Treaty and ultimately, to the statehood of Ohio.

Tecumseh (c. 1768–1813)

Tecumseh (Tikamthi or "Crouching Panther") was a Native American leader from the Shawnee tribe who was opposed to the annexing of his people's lands to the whites. Despite his enemy status, the whites called him the greatest Native American leader in the Northwest. He spent most of his life attempting to build a unified coalition to successfully oppose the disintegration of Native American territories and culture.

Tecumseh founded Prophet's Town as part of his growing Indian Confederation. He continued to demand the return of native lands as well as recruit more forces to join his nation. Forced to move the town further away from the whites, Tecumseh resettled his people at Tippecanoe River in Indiana.

Governor William Henry Harrison of continued to press Tecumseh for more land, but the Shawnee leader refused. Tensions began to mount and Harrison marched troops to Tippecanoe while Tecumseh was gone, attacking and destroying

Prophet's Town. Tecumseh continued to oppose Harrison's forces by siding with the British and defending Canada, but perished in the Battle of Thames in the War of 1812. His death extinguished any life his native coalition might have had.

DID YOU  KNOW?

Tecumseh predicted the New Madrid earthquake, the most violent and destructive earthquake to ever strike North America in recorded history. Tecumseh prophesied several months in advance that the Great Spirit would shake the ground as a sign the whites could be defeated. On December 16, 1811, an enormous earthquake centered in New Madrid, Missouri, shook the entire eastern half of the continent, toppling brick chimneys in Maine and ringing church bells in Canada as well as causing the mighty Mississippi River to run backwards.

Nathaniel Massie (1763–1813)

A surveyor and land speculator, he founded Massie's Station (now Manchester, Ohio), the first American settlement in the Virginian Military District. He also founded the state's first capital, Chillicothe.

Commodore Oliver Hazard Perry (1785–1819)
At age 28, this officer of the United States Navy secured the defense of the Ohio Valley by defeating the British at the Battle of Lake Erie. During the fight, Perry's own ship was destroyed, so he rowed half a mile through heavy gunfire to man another one of his ships. He is famous for his words to General William Henry Harrison: "I have met the enemy and they are ours."

Thomas Worthington (1773–1827)
He was one of a handful of men who encouraged President Thomas Jefferson to make Ohio into a state. One of the state's first senators, he was active in the decision of the United States to send military aid to reinforce the position of Ohio settlers in their opposition to Tecumseh and his forces. Worthington resigned from his position as senator to become governor of Ohio. He spearheaded several progressive initiatives, including state assistance to the poor, prison reform, free public education and the regulation of liquor establishments.

Salmon P. Chase (1808–73)

Salmon Chase served as senator and then governor of Ohio, U.S. treasury secretary under Abraham Lincoln and then chief justice of the United States. However, Chase is best remembered for his resolute anti-slavery stance. He coined the term "Free Soil, Free Labor, Free Men," and was a vigorous and persistent enemy of what he called slave power, the conspiracy of slave owners to seize control of the federal government and thwart the progress of liberty.

Originally from Cornish, New Hampshire, he moved to Cincinnati in 1830 to practice law. He soon established himself as a defender of escaped slaves, so much so that he was dubbed the "Attorney General for Fugitive Slaves."

 Salmon P. Chase established the national banking system and issued the federal government's first paper money. He was the one who chose green as the color of the U.S. paper currency. The Chase Manhattan Bank still bears his name.

George Armstrong Custer (1839–76)

Forever associated with the disastrous defeat at the Battle of Little Bighorn, General Custer nonetheless had numerous victories in several battles, including the Gettysburg Campaign and was the youngest general in the Union army.

Born in New Rumley, he taught school in Ohio before enrolling in the United States Military Academy. Known for pulling pranks, he almost didn't make it through military school because of the demerits he received. He graduated from West Point in 1861 and quickly became known on the battlefield for his acumen and aggressive maneuvering. He would also be known as one of the first publicity hounds, purposely flamboyant and manipulative to draw attention to his reputation. When not fully engaged in battle, his restless nature still got him into trouble with the military. Nonetheless, his record of military successes was one of the finest at the time.

He insisted on going to the Battle of Little Bighorn, where a combination of events led to the annihilation of Custer and his forces, which included his two brothers, his brother-in-law and his nephew.

DID YOU KNOW?

Custer's hobby of stuffing dead animals may have led to his downfall on the fighting field. Taxidermy back then required large amounts of arsenic for the preparation of specimens, and the dangers to humans weren't realized yet, although it was common knowledge that taxidermists always seemed to die young. According to historical accounts, by the time Custer reached the Little Big Horn Battle, he had large of clumps of his hair falling out, and other symptoms of arsenic poisoning. Chances are even if he had survived the battle, he would have most certainly have died shortly thereafter.

Johnny Appleseed (1774—1847)

Johnny Appleseed was born as John Chapman in Massachusetts. Apprenticed to an apple orchardist, John learned the science and art of horticulture at an early age. When the Pennsylvania and Ohio territories opened up, no nurseries had yet been established, so the area lacked orchards and fruit trees for the incoming settlers. John Chapman's family had already moved to Ohio and John, seeing that an important food source was not yet available, decided to dedicate himself to filling the void. He collected apple seeds from cider presses in Pennsylvania and started working his way west to the Ohio River valley, giving away and selling apple seeds and saplings to settlers heading west. As he traveled, he planted seeds where he could; establishing 1200 acres of his own nurseries as well as helping hundreds of other people to start their own. Known for his extraordinary kindness and earnest interest in nature conservation; he was considered by Native Americans as a great medicine man. He dressed in a coffee sack, ragged pants and a tin mush pan for a hat, yet he was destined to become the stuff of legends—and has.

WOMEN WHO MADE WAVES

Annie Oakley (1860—1926)

The first female superstar, Annie Oakley was a sharpshooter and exhibition shooter. Born Phoebe Ann Mosey in North Star, her childhood was marked by poverty and tragedy. With her mother widowed and her family forced from their home because of a fire, Annie began hunting at the age of nine to support her starving siblings. She also spent time in servitude to a local family, where she was mentally and physically abused. As a result of her dire circumstances, she never received a real chance to go to school and would achieve a more complete education later in life.

Her reputation as a skilled shooter began to spread, and in the spring of 1881, a local hotel owner by the name of Jack Frost took up show marksman Frank Butler's bet that he could beat any local shooter. He arranged for Annie to shoot against Frank for $100. Frank lost the match and the bet, but won the heart of Annie. They married and joined Buffalo Bill's Wild West Show where she would perform for kings, queens, presidents and audiences around the world. She continued performing into her sixties, but also quietly directed extensive energy into philanthropic endeavors such as women's rights. She died of pernicious anemia in 1926. Her husband Frank, devastated by her death, died 18 days later. It was discovered at that time that Annie had spent her entire fortune on charities.

Victoria Woodhull

Born in Hamlet in 1838, this outspoken woman became the first woman in history to be nominated as a presidential candidate. Supported by the Equal Rights Party in 1872, she championed the suffragette movement as well as other liberties for women. Because her followers couldn't vote for her, she obviously lost the election, but she gained the attention of media everywhere, securing her spot in history. She died in 1927.

Alice and Phoebe Cary

Sisters who were at the forefront of the literary movement of their time, Alice (1820–71) and Phoebe (1824–71) became known for their works of poetry. Born on a farm a few miles north of Cincinnati, both sisters had solid writing talent and were soon recognized for it. First published in the *Cincinnati Sentinel* in 1847, the sisters would have their works published continuously throughout the rest of the country with much acclaim. Edgar Allen Poe, Horace Greeley and John Greenleaf Whittier counted themselves among their fans.

In a daring move for their gender, Alice and Phoebe moved to New York City in 1850 and set up a literary parlor for intellectuals, artists and social reformers. Among the regular visitors were P.T. Barnum, Mary Booth, editor of *Harper's Bazaar*, Elizabeth and Richard Stoddard and many more writers, actors and philanthropists.

The sisters died within six months of each other and almost every major newspaper in the country carried their obituaries.

Mary Ann Bickerdyke (1817–1901)

Born in Knox County in 1817, she became the nation's first war nurse as she tended to Union soldiers. The only woman allowed in General Sherman's camps, she became a hero to them, and they cheered her as they would a general when she appeared on the scene. She performed all duties from brewing coffee to assisting in amputations, always comforting and aiding "her boys," as she called them. By the end of the war, she had co-founded 300 hospitals and had tended to the wounded on 19 different battlefields. At Sherman's request, she rode at the head of the XV Corps in the Grand Review in Washington at the end of the war. She died in 1901.

Florence Ellinwood Allen

Florence Allen (1884–1966) specialized in breaking the barriers for women in the legal profession. Born in Utah and raised in Cleveland, she earned a BA as well as an MA degree from Western Reserve University and was elected to Phi Beta Kappa. She became the only woman in a law class of 100 at the University of Chicago. In 1922 she was elected to the Ohio Supreme Court and was appointed to the United States Court of Appeals for the Sixth Circuit by President Franklin D. Roosevelt in 1934. In 1959, she became the first woman to be chief judge of a United States Appeals Court. She was also active in human rights work and published an autobiography called, *To Do Justly*.

WARS AND CONFLICTS

Yellow Creek Massacre 1774

Chief Logan had been friends with whites for as long as he could remember. In fact his name had come from James Logan, a Pennsylvania official that Chief Logan's father had worked with and whom Logan admired. Chief Logan, or Logan the Mingo, maintained friendly relations with the settlers moving in from eastern Pennsylvania and Virginia. But all that would come to an abrupt and brutal end on May 3, 1774. Tensions had been mounting between other groups of whites and natives, and when a tavern owner at Yellow Creek was warned of imminent danger to him and his family by vengeful natives, a call for help went out. Twenty-two year old Daniel Greathouse, a settler in colonial Virginia, responded by organizing a party of 21 men.

They descended upon Chief Logan's family, who happened to be in the area. Greathouse and his men, not realizing these natives were friends and not enemies, murdered Logan's brother, mother, daughter, sister and cousin, as well as seven other friends and family. The victims were scalped, a signal to the aboriginals that the whites had declared war.

In turn, this event sparked what would become known as Dunmore's War, a war between the Colony of Virginia and the Native American peoples of the Shawnee and Mingo. Dunmore's army eventually compelled the two tribes to agree to a peace treaty, but legend has it that Logan refused the offer and instead gave a speech that would become famous. It was printed throughout colonial newspapers and Thomas Jefferson reprinted it in his book, *Notes on the State of Virginia*.

"I appeal to any white man to say, if ever he entered Logan's cabin hungry and he gave him not meat; if ever he came cold and naked and he clothed him not. During the course of the last long and bloody war, Logan remained idle in his cabin, an advocate for peace. Such was my love for the whites, that my countrymen pointed as they passed and said, Logan is the friend of the white men. I have even thought to live with you but for the injuries of one man...the last spring, in cold blood and unprovoked, murdered all the relations of Logan, not sparing even my women and children....Who is there to mourn for Logan? Not one."

Chief Logan would later join the American Revolution against the Americans and would be killed in 1780. A monument to Logan is located at the Elm State Park in Pickaway County. The text of Logan's famous speech is inscribed upon it.

Gnadenhutten Massacre 1782

During the Revolutionary War, many aboriginal people were divided about what side to take. Some supported the British while others allied themselves with the rebelling colonists. Some, like the Christian Munsee American Indians, took no side at all, preferring to be neutral and unarmed, and work and live alongside the Moravian missionaries.

In 1781, British-allied troops suspected the Munsees and Moravians of aiding the American side, so they forcibly removed them from their villages and relocated them at Captive Town near the Sandusky River. Conditions there were less than ideal. The Munsees began to starve and in 1782, around 100 of them returned to their former villages to harvest the crops they were forced to leave behind. A raiding party of 160 Pennsylvania militiamen happened upon the Munsees and accused them of criminal activity. They truthfully denied the charges, but to no avail. Among the 96 murdered and scalped were 28 men, 29 women and 39 children. Two boys, one of whom was scalped, survived to tell of the massacre.

The Toledo War

The Toledo War (also known as the Ohio-Michigan War), fought between 1835 and 1836, was mostly a bloodless boundary dispute between Ohio and the adjoining territory of Michigan. The dispute originated from varying interpretations of conflicting state and federal legislation, passed between 1787 and 1805. This caused the governments of Ohio and Michigan to both claim sovereignty over a 468-square mile region along the border, now known as the Toledo Strip.

In 1835, both states sent forces to opposite sides of the Maumee River near Toledo, but very little happened between the two sides. The single military confrontation of the "war" ended with no casualties and only one report of a slightly wounded Michigan sheriff. Michigan finally gave up the fight when it accepted a compromise from Congress that gave them three-quarters of the Upper Peninsula in exchange for the Toledo Strip.

WHAT'S IN A NAME?

Columbus

Named for the famed explorer of 1492, Columbus is the capital of Ohio as well as the state's largest city. It was officially founded on February 14, 1812 at the convergence of the Scioto and Olentangy Rivers as more of a political compromise than anything else. Previously, the capital had been located in different quadrants: Chillicothe, Zanesville and these Chillicothe again. Columbus offered a central location that stopped complaints of geographical favoritism.

DID YOU KNOW?

In 1875, C.D. Firestone founded the Columbus Buggy Company, one of 20 buggy manufacturers in the city, a fact that contributed to Columbus' nickname "Buggy Capital of the World." Firestone's nephew, Harvey S. Firestone, would work for his uncle's company before founding the Firestone Tire and Rubber Company, the first global maker of automobile tires.

Cleveland

This city was named after General Moses Cleaveland, who oversaw the layout of what is now the city's downtown area. Founded in 1796, the city was incorporated in 1814 and changed its name in 1831, when the "a" was dropped so the name could fit in the newspaper's masthead.

Cincinnati

Originally named Losantiville by John Filson, author of *The Adventures of Daniel Boone* (who also happened to be the land surveyor of the area), the name was changed by the Northwest Territory governor to Cincinnati in honor of the Roman general Cincinnatus.

 Cincinnati was the first city in the U.S. to have a full-time paid fire department as well the first city in the world to use steam-powered fire engines.

Toledo

Named after the city in Spain, Toledo has historically also been known as "Frog Town" because of its proximity to a glacially created wetland known as the Great Black Swamp. Home to actors Jamie Farr (Max Klinger from M*A*S*H) and Katie Holmes (a.k.a. Mrs. Tom Cruise) as well as feminist Gloria Steinem, Toledo is also known for constructing the first building covered in glass.

The Great Black Swamp became a real problem during a border dispute known as the Toledo War of 1835-36. Michigan and Ohio militias had set out to meet each other in battle, only to find the Great Black Swamp so impossible to pass through that they were never able to find each other to fight.

Akron

Named after the Greek word meaning "summit," Akron was founded at the geographical high point of the Ohio and Erie Canal. Originally founded as a settlement to provide resources for the canals and subsequent industries that relied on water power, Akron became a key player for the coal, railroad and manufacturing industries.

 The first automobile police patrol wagon was used in Akron in 1899.

Dayton

Named after Jonathon Dayton, a signer of the U.S. Constitution, this city showcases a star-studded history as well as playing a major role in politics, aerospace and engineering. The Wright Brothers, African-American poet Paul Laurence Dunbar and entrepreneur John Patterson hail from Dayton. Several inventions call Dayton home, too, such as pop top beverage cans, the movie projector, the parachute, the cash register and the stepladder, to name a few. The Dayton Agreement—the peace accord between Bosnia and the former country of Yugoslavia—was negotiated and signed at Wright-Patterson Air Force Base near Dayton.

DID YOU  KNOW?

The first All-American Soap Box Derby was held in Dayton in 1934.

Parma

A suburb of Cleveland, Parma was founded in 1826 as part of Parma Township. Although named after the Italian city of the same name, Parma was known for its mostly Polish population, even more so after becoming the standard butt of Polish jokes by local television talk show hosts in the 1960s and 1970s.

Youngstown

The city, founded in 1797, was named for a settler by the name of John Young, who not only surveyed the land that was soon to be a city but also bought it so he could set up a sawmill and gristmill.

Canton

Say "Canton" to any pro-football enthusiast and most likely they will respond "Pro Football Hall of Fame." Founded in 1805 and named after a plantation in Maryland, Canton was the city that founded the American Professional Football League, now known as the National Football League, or the NFL.

Lorain

Seated in the county named after Lorraine, France, this city was originally called Charleston when founded in 1807. Reincorporated in 1874 after surviving a severe economic downturn, the city renamed itself with the name of the county that it is located in. Lorain was also the birthplace and child-hood home of African-American author and Nobel Prize for Literature recipient, Toni Morrison.

Marysville

Named for founder Samuel Cuthbertson's daughter, Marysville was established in 1816 and grew quickly by specializing in agri-cultural products and services. The city has developed into an important manufacturing center for several companies, includ-ing Honda of America. Marysville is also the birthplace of General Robert S. Beightler, the World War II commander who accepted the surrender of General Yamashita and his forces in the Philippines.

Washington Court House

This city's name is a relative newcomer to the name game. Established in 1810, the residents named it after the first presi-dent. The official name, until 2002, was "The City of Washington," but to avoid confusion with another similarly named city, they re-chartered the name to "The City of Washington Court House."

Ravenna
Named after the city of Ravenna, Italy, this town was home to Jesse Grant, father of the 18th President of the United States, Ulysses S. Grant.

Xenia

Founded in 1803, this town was named after the Greek word meaning "hospitality." This area was referred to by the Shawnee Indians as "the place of the devil winds" because of its history of violent weather. This proved itself especially true in 1974 when an F5 tornado sliced a path through this town, killing 34 people, injuring over 1100 and leaving nearly 10,000 homeless.

Bucyrus
The name is a combination of the words "beautiful" and "Cyrus" after Cyrus the Great (a renowned king of Persia ca. 590 BC). Founded in 1822, this city is the first in the U.S. to use this name. Several full and partial remains of mastodons have been discovered in the area.

Bellefontaine

The area that is now the city of Bellefontaine was first known as Blue Jacket's Town, named after the Shawnee warrior Blue Jacket. The settlement was officially established in 1820 and named "Bellefontaine," which means "beautiful spring," for the limestone springs that were once in the area.

Bellefontaine became the first town in America to have the first street paved with concrete. It is also home to the famous McKinley Street, the world's shortest street at a length of 15 feet.

UNUSUAL NAMES

Knockemstiff

It's a strange name whose history has been forgotten, but there are a few theories as to how this town got its moniker. Situated in southern Ohio in Ross County, Knockemstiff is little more than a ghost town. It is located among the Appalachian foot-hills, where running moonshine used to be the main industry. The other main occupation in the town back then apparently was brawling. Both activities play into the premise of the origin of the town's name. A more humorous story tells the tale of a wife seeking to change her husband's cheating ways. She asked her preacher what she could do. His reply? "Go home and knock 'em stiff."

Pee Pee

This township got its smirk-inducing name from Irish settler Peter Patrick who had carved his initials into a tree. Legend has it that the local Indian population didn't care for his woodcarving talent and chased him out of the area. His initials, however, remained firmly intact and now grace both the township and a nearby creek.

Ai

The shortest name of any town in Ohio, it earned it the hard way—through reputation. Located 20 miles west of Toledo, this little town at one time had a dozen saloons and more than enough thieves and other apparently morally challenged folks to keep them in business. Such good business, in fact, that people in the surrounding county remarked the yet-unnamed town would suffer the same fate as Ai, the wicked town destroyed by Joshua in the Old Testament. The name stuck, although the saloons and scoundrels have met a fate far less dramatic than predicted…by fading into the pages of history.

Fly

There are a couple of theories as to how this town was named. One involves pesky insects bothering folks at a meeting convened for the purpose of naming the town; another story has it that a cranky federal postal official helped name the town. This particular official was asked by a local congressman to grant the tiny municipality a post office—a task more troublesome than the postal official thought worthy. Grudgingly giving into the demand, he approved a post office but listed the town as Flyspeck (as in "a flyspeck on a map") just for spite. Outraged, the congressman promised repercussions if amends were not made. The postal official, still cantankerous, agreed to make some sort of change, so he shortened the town name to Fly. The official stuck to his word and the name stuck to the town.

Alert

This community also earned its name from reputation—its literary reputation. Back in 1821, a library known as the Literary Association of Morgan and Crosby townships began distributing books and news items to the farmers and townsfolk of the area. The library's activities became known in the corner of the state and gave the municipality the character of being an "alert" population, as in aware of and attentive to the events of the world. Not one to pass up a good nickname, the town chose the adjective for its official name.

Brokensword

Named for one of the many gruesome events in Ohio's early history, Brokensword is named the final chapter of Colonel William Crawford's life. A soldier and surveyor, he had already retired from active duty when General George Washington called him up to lead a contingent of men to exterminate the natives along the Muskingum River in Ohio. Outnumbered, the battle went badly and Colonel Crawford was captured.

To prevent himself from being killed with his own weapon, Crawford stabbed his sword into the bank of the river and broke the blade. Undeterred, the natives tortured and burnt him at the stake. In time, however, the native population was driven out and the subsequent settlement named Brokensword, in reference to Crawford's act.

Blue Ball

Recently annexed by nearby Middletown, this burg's unusual name dates back to when horsepower referred to how many horses you had hitched to your wagon. Originally called Guilford, it was a stage coach stop between Dayton and Cincinnati that apparently needed more business. Since most stage coach drivers were illiterate, they could not read the signs in town that advertised their pubs and passed by Guilford. Back then, most drivers relied on an old medieval reference of a blue-colored sphere to spot hospitality. Sensing the need for some good old fashioned marketing, the town voted in 1862 to change its name to Blue Ball and placed an appropriately corresponding landmark where the drivers could see it. It worked and a modern replica of the original blue ball still exists today.

Twinsburg

This town started at as Millsville in 1817, but that changed when identical twins Moses and Aaron Wilcox bought 400 acres of land and began selling it off in smaller parcels with the request that the town name be changed to Twinsburg. Residents complied, helped along by the twins' offer of $20.00 toward the construction of a new school if they renamed the town. In 1976, Twinsburg held the first yearly festival for twins called Twin Days. Since then, the festival has grown to attract twins, triplets and other multiple siblings from all over and has become the word's largest annual gathering of its kind.

Nicknames

- Akron—Rubber City of the World; Home of the Soap Box Derby

- Dayton—Gem City; Birthplace of Aviation; High School Reunion Capital of the U.S.

- Cincinnati—Porkopolis; Queen City of the West; City of Seven Hills; Paris of America; Blue Chip City

- Columbus—Information Capital of the World; Arch City; Buggy Capital of the World

- Cleveland—Rock 'n' Roll Capital of the World; Pierogi Capital of America

- Anna—Earthquake Capital of Ohio

- Urichsville—Clay Center of the World

- Zanesville—Y-Bridge City

Foreign Names

Visit the world's capitals without ever leaving the state: start in Rome (Adams County), make your way to London (Madison County), hop over to Dublin (Franklin County), then enjoy Geneva (Fairfield County), Paris (Stark County), Lisbon (Columbiana County) and Amsterdam (Jefferson County). I would also recommend seeing Berlin (Holmes County), Athens (Athens County) and Warsaw (Coshocton County) to round out the trip nicely.

COUNTY CLAIM TO FAME

A Rundown of Ohio's 88

Ohio boasts 88 interesting counties, as you read below:

☞ Adams County is named in honor of President John Adams. Ironically, Ohio was the birthplace of eight presidents, but Adams was not among them.

☞ Vermont hero Ethan Allen—one time leader of the citizen's militia group the Green Mountain Boys—is the namesake of Ohio's Allen County.

☞ Hot air balloons fill the sky during Ashland County's most unique annual festival, BalloonFest. The event is typically held near the July 4th weekend.

☛ Ohio's largest county is Ashtabula County. With 16 covered bridges and 15 wineries, the county calls itself the "covered bridge and winery capital of Ohio."

☛ Athens County was established in 1805 and named after, you guessed it, Athens, Greece.

☛ Auglaize County's second courthouse, replacing the first one built in 1851, was erected in 1893 for the princely sum of $259,481. It continues to serve the county to this day.

☛ The Blaine Bridge of Belmont County, built in 1828, was named "the Ohio Bicentennial Bridge" and is the oldest of its kind in the state.

☛ The War of 1812 and General Jacob Brown were immortalized in the naming of Brown County.

☛ Butler County is home to the seventh oldest public university in the nation—Miami University.

☛ Charles Carroll of Carrollton was the "last surviving signer of the Declaration of Independence." Carroll County is named in his honour.

☛ Champaign County actually derived its name from the French word for "plain" because of its flat countryside, but the county's motto is a little more flamboyant: "The Champaign of Counties."

☛ In its first census, Clark County had a population of 9533 people. By 2000, that number had increased to 144,742.

☛ Clermont County was established in December of 1800, but its first village, Williamsburg, was established in 1796.

☛ Since 2004, Clinton County has hosted an annual Quaker Genealogy and History Conference.

☛ Christopher Columbus was immortalized in the naming of Columbiana County in 1829.

☛ Crawford County was named after soldier and surveyor William Crawford. In 1982, the site where he was burned at the stake was added to the National Register of Historic Places.

☛ With a population of 1,393,978, according to 2000 Census figures, Cuyahoga County is the most populated county in Ohio. Cuyahoga is a Native American word meaning "crooked river."

☛ Darke and Stark counties are two of very few counties in the entire nation to have eight county neighbors.

☛ Of the 414 square miles (1073 square kilometers) that make up Defiance County, only three square miles (eight square kilometers or 0.73 percent) is water.

☛ According to U.S. Census Bureau's 2004 population estimates, Delaware County is Ohio's fastest growing county and 11th nation-wide.

☛ The word "Erie" means "wildcat" in the language of the Erie Indians, and the county was named in their honor.

☞ There's no mistaking what folks in Fairfield are proud of. The county was formed on December 9, 1800 and named after their beautiful "fair fields."

☞ There are 10 townships in the largely rural county of Fayette.

☞ The average temperature in Franklin County is about 56°F. If that's a tad chilly or a bit on the warm side for you, don't worry. The county's weather motto is "Wait five minutes, it'll change." Franklin County is also home of Columbus, the state capital city.

☞ Fulton County boasts a motto of its own, "I will find a way or I will make one." A fitting salute, considering this county is named after steamboat inventor Robert Fulton.

☞ At 31,069, the entire population of Gallia County isn't much larger than a small city.

☞ "Geauga" in Geauga County is a Native American word meaning "raccoon."

☞ Old Chillicothe (or Old Town) is thought to be the oldest settlement in Greene County. It was Ohio's first capital city and its statehouse was the state's first stone building.

☞ Guernsey County's first residents were a handful of Delaware Indians. Numbering about 50, they lived in houses south of Will's Creek.

☞ With 130 schools under their mandate, the Roman Catholic Archdiocese of Cincinnati operates the "ninth largest private system in the United States" in Ohio's Hamilton County.

☞ Unlike many other counties whose first settlers were French in origin, most of Hancock County's first pioneers originated from Pennsylvania.

☛ About 440 square miles of "old Indian territory" went into the forming of Hardin County in 1820, but it wasn't until 1833 that the county was formally organized.

☛ Harrison County lays claim to a number of notable citizens. Among them are: American Civil War commander George Custer; Congress representative and part-author of the 14th amendment to the Constitution John Bingham; and none other than the actor who melted hearts as Rhett Butler in *Gone with the Wind*, Clark Gable.

☛ Located in the northwestern portion of the state, the area that makes up Henry County was once described as "The Great Black Swamp."

☛ Pride in their colorful fall foliage has led folks in Hillsboro County to warn visitors to wear their sunglasses when visiting in the fall.

☛ Though not all agree, some scholars believe "Hocking" is a Delaware Indian word meaning "bottle." The description was used to name the Hocking River and where the county derived its name.

☛ White settlers first came to Holmes County between 1809 and 1810, and the first white baby born there was one Hannah Butler. She was born on February 4, 1810.

☛ Huron County derived its name from the Huron Indians.

☛ Soldier, geologist and explorer John Wesley Powell is considered by many "Jackson County's most famous native son." He is credited with being "the first man to navigate the Grand Canyon of the Colorado River."

☛ One of Ohio's oldest, Jefferson County was the fifth to be established, on July 29, 1797.

☞ In 1869, the Ringwalt Store first opened its doors for business in Knox County. It didn't hang up the "closed" sign for the final time until 1990, 121 years later.

☞ Lake County was named for the fact that it borders the southeastern corner of Lake Erie. Covering an area of only 232 square miles, it is the state's smallest county.

☞ Lawrence County is well known for its wealth of natural resources, especially timber and iron. Perhaps this is why the county seat of Ironton, known for its iron production, is so named.

☞ The salt licks located throughout the area provided the inspiration for the naming of Licking County.

☞ At an elevation of 1549 feet, Campbell Hill is the highest elevation in Ohio. It is located just northeast of Bellefontaine in Logan County.

☞ Lorain County is quite likely the land—or rather water— of my heart. Covering a total area of 923 square miles (2392 square kilometers), 46.64 percent or 431 square miles (1115 square kilometers) of it is water.

☞ Border disputes marred the establishment of Lucas County and on August 20, 1794, General Anthony Wayne led an assault against the aboriginals inhabiting the county's southern border. Known as the Battle of Fallen Timbers, the dispute ended with settlement expanding into the northwest.

☞ Eighty-eight percent of the land making up Madison County is made up of farms. The county's prolific soybean and corn production is fourth highest in the state.

☛ Demographically speaking, women rule the roost in Mahoning County. According to the 2000 Census, there were "91.40 males for every 100 females."

☛ In another largely rural area, Marion County's average income in 1999 was estimated at $22,000 per person and a staggering 12 percent of the population was thought to be living in poverty.

☛ With most communities anchored by a town square surrounded by "authentic Victorian buildings," the visitor's bureau in Medina County boasts "some of the most beautiful historic architecture" in the state.

☛ Less than one percent of Meigs County's 429 square miles consists of urban areas. Less than one percent—0.68 percent actually—of this area is made up of water.

☞ Agriculture is the primary industry in Mercer County; it leads the state in hog production and is second in corn production.

☞ Although a primarily rural area, Miami County saw a population increase of about 6.1 percent between 1990 and 2000.

☞ Swiss immigrants to the area played a major role in establishing Monroe County. According to its official government website, the county's motto might be "Ohio's Rising Star," but many folks also refer to it as the "Switzerland of Ohio."

☞ It was in an inconspicuous bicycle shop in Dayton, the Montgomery County seat, where Wilbur and Orville Wright designed and developed their first airplane to successfully fly.

☞ In 1790, Big Bottom was the first community established in Morgan County. Sadly, 12 settlers were killed there in an altercation with the Native American population. The event is known as the Big Bottom Massacre.

☞ Quakers, also known as the Society of Friends, made up a significant portion of the population of early settlers to Morrow County. Perhaps it was the frugal nature of its residents, but people in this county purchased more Victory bonds during World War I than any other Ohio county.

☞ The world of art pottery has a lot to be grateful for when it comes to the contributions of Muskingum County. In 1890, Samuel A. Weller established a pottery manufacturing plant there. Within 15 years it employed 500 workers and by 1910 Weller's plant was responsible for producing more pottery than any other manufacturer in the world. The county was also once home to author Zane Grey, known mainly for writing books romanticizing the old West.

☛ North America's first oil well was discovered in Noble County in 1814. It was the last of Ohio's 88 counties to establish itself in 1851.

☛ Ottawa County was formed in 1840, but it took 60 years of legal wrangling before Port Clinton was officially (and for the fifth time) chosen as the site of its county courthouse.

☛ Paulding County's motto is "No Compromise," which stems from an uprising over a part of a canal system that had been abandoned. Fed up with the state's lack of interest in taking care of this malaria-producing reservoir, locals dynamited and pick-axed their way through the dikes, causing significant damage to the system and forcing the state to call out its militia for the first in time in its short history.

☛ Perry County has the dubious distinction of being considered "one of the poorest counties in the state."

☛ Folks in Pickaway County are obviously quite proud of their corner of the state. Their county motto is "The Pick of Ohio."

☛ Pike County is named after Zebulon Pike, the explorer who discovered Colorado's high point, Pike's Peak.

☛ While Portage County is predominantly rural, agriculture is only the fifth-largest employer. Leading the county is manufacturing.

☛ An Ohio law states that in 2007, all properties in Preble County must be reappraised.

☛ Organizers call the annual fair in Putnam County "A Blue Ribbon Event."

☛ It's no surprise that agriculture is one of the prime industries in Richland County. After all, the county was named after the "rich land" found throughout the region.

☛ Ross County is geographically the second largest county in Ohio. It covers 687 square miles of land.

☛ Rutherford B. Hayes, the country's 19th president, was born in Sandusky County.

☛ The area making up Scioto County was once part of neighboring Adams County. It officially formed on March 24, 1903.

☛ The Seneca Indians were saluted in the naming of Seneca County.

☛ The highest elevation in Shelby County and the surrounding area is Loramie's summit. It measures 378 feet above sea level.

☛ During any federal election, all eyes are typically on Ohio—and more particularly on Stark County. This county's voting record has so closely tracked the winner of U.S. presidential elections, it is considered a reliable indicator as to the outcome. Candidates visit the region frequently during an election year, and large media outlets take care to concentrate on Stark County's citizens and their political opinions during that time.

☛ Akron is located in Summit County. Because B.F. Goodrich, Firestone Tire and Rubber and the Goodyear Tire and Rubber companies all make their home there, Akron is known as "The Rubber Capital of the World."

☛ Trumbull County was named after Connecticut Governor Jonathan Trumbull because he once owned much of the county's land.

☛ Schoenbrunn was Tuscarawas County's first settlement. Founded in 1772, it was the "first protestant settlement in Ohio."

- Marysville isn't just Union's County seat, it's also where William Henry Harrison's "Log Cabin" campaign began.

- Van Wert County is home to the first county-wide public library in the nation, the Brumback Library.

- The county with the smallest population in the state is Vinton County.

- General and Dr. Joseph Warren died at the Battle of Bunker Hill. Warren County is named in his memory.

- Washington County is the oldest county in the state. In case you were wondering, yes it was named in honor of George Washington.

- Wayne County farmers rank first in the state in several production areas: oats, hay, cattle and dairy.

☛ The population of Williams County, between 1990 and 2000, has increased by six percent.

☛ Fort Meigs was established in Wood County during the War of 1812. Its prime responsibility was to protect the state "from a British invasion from Canada."

☛ Loosely translated, Wyandot means "around the plains" or "dwellers on the peninsula." The word comes from the Wyandot Indians and Wyandot County is named in their honor.

DRUGS, BOOZE AND ALL THINGS INDULGENT

"Yeah, but this is Ohio. I mean, if you don't have a brewski in your hand, you might as well be wearing a dress."
—Quoted from the movie *Heathers* (1989)

Putting the "High" in Ohio

Because of its well-ordered and maintained interstate highway system, easy drug distribution and access is a problem in Ohio, with northern parts of the state classified as High Intensity Drug Trafficking Areas by the Office of National Drug Control Policy. The warmer climate and rural areas of the southern part of Ohio lend themselves well to marijuana cultivation. It's not unusual to hear of federal agents seizing rows of marijuana planted in between rows of corn or to read of the arrest of a person growing reefer alongside Roma tomatoes in their garden.

Hempfest

Organized annually by the Ohio State University Students for Sensible Drug Policy, this event showcases speakers, politicians, activists, musicians and food vendors for the purpose of legitimizing hemp. This festival will mark its 21st year in 2007 and continues to draw fanatics, skeptics and everyone in between.

Pioneering Pornography

Dayton holds the dubious and salacious honor of playing host to the beginnings of Larry Flynt's career in pornography and strip clubs. Larry opened his first strip club there in 1970 and soon expanded to include Columbus, Toledo, Akron and Cleveland. He started Hustler magazine in 1974 and the rest, as they say, is eyebrow-raising history.

Ohio's Fine Wine

Ohio is one of the top ten states in wine production in the nation. The trend was started in the early 1800s by Nicholas Longworth, who planted semi-sweet Catawba grapes, resulting in wines that put Ohio on the map. In fact, prior to the Civil War, Ohio was considered America's most important wine-producing state. However, war and crop disease wiped out southern Ohio's wine industry, only to have it replaced in the north, along Lake Erie. The lake's unique micro-climate, perfect for grapes, coupled with new, disease-resistant grapes led to a wine boom in the 1900s. While it would take some time before Ohio became recognized for its talent in wine-making, it is now competitive on a national scale and ranks fourth in number of wineries and sixth in wine production.

 Nicholas Longworth produced the nation's first champagne.

Spirited Sales

In 2006, Ohio's consumption of spirits containing more than 21 percent alcohol by volume topped $638.8 million. That equals 9.9 million gallons of alcohol!

DID YOU KNOW?

The Beer Barrel Saloon of Put-In-Bay, South Bass Island, is home to the world's longest bar as recorded by the *Guinness Book of World Records*. It is 405 feet and 10 inches long.

GENERAL LIFESTYLE

Active Ohio

While the weather can be changeable, Ohioans are consistent in what they like to do: they like to eat (a side effect of living in an agricultural economy), to shop and to walk. Chances are you will find all three interests combined for your convenience no matter where you go. During the cold and inhospitable winter months, you'll find most of the walking done inside warm and comfortable shopping malls. For the other three seasons, Ohioans move outside to places like the Flats in Cleveland, the Short North in Columbus and Newport on the Levee in Cincinnati. They also take advantage of over 4700 miles of hiking trails available throughout the state as well as walking through the many different festivals, celebrations and fairs that occur throughout the year. Over 172.2 million trips were taken to or within Ohio during 2005, resulting in $33.1 billion— that's billion—dollars spent on recreation and tourism activities. That's a lot of walking, shopping and eating!

Ohio has other activities and attractions as well. Biking, boating, skiing, rock climbing, horseback riding and canoeing are among just a few of the options available. When you have both flat open spaces and hilly terrain situated in between lakes and rivers, the possibilities are practically endless.

Alternative Lifestyle

Ohio has the largest and perhaps the most active gay community between Chicago and Washington D.C. In the March 2007 issue of *Advocate Magazine*, Columbus is among cities voted the most diverse in the country, and is considered a "Top 10 Best Place for Gays and Lesbians to Live in America." This city's lively and unpretentious culture is a blend of the influence of the Ohio State University's 51,000 students, the presence of numerous art galleries and several neighborhoods known for their chic, urban individuality.

Simple Lifestyle

The Amish are a Christian denomination in the United States and Canada (Ontario and Manitoba) known for plain dress and limited use of modern conveniences. The Amish separate themselves from mainstream society for religious reasons: they speak a German dialect; they have either no or very limited use of electricity and cars; they do not join the military; and they do not accept financial assistance from the government.

Although very little official research on the Amish and Mennonite communities of Ohio has been conducted, the state claims the largest population of these religious communities in the world.

WAGES, EMPLOYMENT AND TAXES

Could You Raise My Allowance Please?

Ohio lags slightly behind the rest of the nation when it comes to wages. People in Ohio were paid an average of $18.00 per hour in 2005 while the national average is $18.62 per hour. One reason for this gap is that Ohio's minimum wage has been stuck at $5.15 an hour for 15 years. The state voted in November 2006 to increase the minimum wage $6.85, so hopefully the average wage in Ohio will be seeing a better future in 2007 and beyond.

An Above Average Report Card

According to the 2007 Development Report Card published by the Corporation for Enterprise Development (CFED), a non-profit economic think-tank, Ohio has slightly higher than average rankings for economic best practices. When compared to the rest of the nation, Ohio ranks in the top 25 for:

☞ federal and private research and development

☞ number of scientists and engineers with doctorates

☞ royalties and licenses issued

The state ranked in the top 15 for creating new businesses.

Jobs and Unemployment

Unemployment in Ohio decreased in the year 2006, good news considering the state's unemployment rate was a little bit above the national numbers.

For 2006, Ohio's unemployment rate stood at 5.5 percent, compared to 5.9 percent in 2005. Columbus had the lowest unemployment rate at 4.7 percent, while Cleveland had the highest at 5.4 percent. Cincinnati was in the middle at 5.2 percent. In comparison, the U.S. average unemployment rate was 4.6 percent.

Gross Domestic Product

Ohio's Gross Domestic Product for 2005 was $441 billion, making the state the seventh largest state economy. Ohio's leading industry was the manufacturing sector, which ranks 3rd in the nation for its gross domestic product. The state led the rest of the country in production of fabricated metals, plastics, rubber, electrical equipment and appliances. Ohio is also a top contender as a producer of steel, cars and trucks.

DID YOU  KNOW?

The Honda Motor Company has been ranked by CNN Money as the most fuel-efficient auto company in the U.S. Honda opened its first U.S. plant in Ohio in 1979 and now employs over 16,000 people in the state.

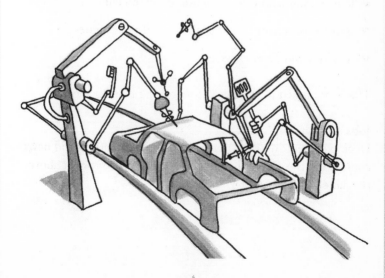

Technology Oriented

It is interesting to note that Ohio's companies are heavy on the technology side of things. A recent survey by Battelle Science and Technology International found that Ohio has a 14 percent higher concentration of technology operations than the rest of the nation.

Farmer Friendly

Also not to be forgotten is the agricultural side of the state. While Ohio ranked 13th overall in the nation in net farm income, it came in 1st for Swiss cheese production, 2nd for egg production and 3rd for tomatoes. Anyone want a cheese and tomato omelet?

DID YOU KNOW?

If Ohio were a country instead of a state, it would rank 26th in the world for the largest economy. That would place it ahead of Switzerland!

Ohio's Top Employers

Ohio's top 10 employers for 2006, as ranked by the number of people employed in the state:

Rank	Employer	Employees	Sector
1	Wal-Mart Stores	50,000	retail general merchandise
2	Cleveland Clinic Health System	34,800	health
3	Kroger Company	34,130	retail food stores
4	University Hospitals Health System	25,000	health
5	Ohio State University	24,400	education and health
6	Catholic Healthcare Partners	23,000	health
7	General Motors Corporation	19,300	manufacture motor vehicles
8	Wright-Patterson Air Force Base	18,250	government air force base
9	JP Morgan Chase & Co.	17,000	finance bank
10	General Electric Company	17,000	aerospace/electrical equipment

The Healthcare Industry

It should not come as a surprise that so many people are employed by the healthcare industry in Ohio. The state is recognized for its assets in that industry, specifically because of several flagship hospitals such as The Cleveland Clinic and the University Hospitals of Cleveland, with its Rainbow Babies and Children's Hospital ranked among the top ten best in the country.

So, Where Do You Work?

Ohio is a lot like the rest of the nation when it comes to where people work. In fact, the only major difference is in the manufacturing industry, where 17 percent of Ohioans work rather than the national average of 13 percent.

Here's where Ohioans go to work every day:

- 12 percent: management, business and finance
- 16 percent: service industry
- 18 percent: construction trade
- 19 percent: professional and related occupations
- 25 percent: sales or in an office-type environment

Median Income

In 1980, the median income for Ohioans was $25,773. Ten years later, Ohio saw its median income rise to $30,013. In 2000, Ohio's median income rose again to $42,962. Happily, the upward trend continued in 2005 with the median income rising to $44,203.

Taxes

Ohio, like most other states, relies on property taxes, income taxes and consumption taxes for its tax revenues. The income tax levies higher taxes on higher incomes and less on lower incomes so the system can remain relatively balanced among the three.

In 2004, Ohio's combined state and local taxes totaled 11 percent of total income versus the U.S. average of 10.4 percent. On the other hand, Ohio had low to average sales taxes and property taxes, when compared to the rest of the country.

DID YOU KNOW?

Ohioans will have to work for the first four months of the year (119 days, to be exact) just to earn enough money to pay the federal, state and local taxes for 2007. In comparison, residents of Connecticut will have to work 140 days to reach that point; Oklahomans will have to work only 102 days.

The Cost of Living That Is Not So Costly

Ohio's cost of living is very attractive. It averages 5.5 percent lower than the rest of the country, meaning what you earn will go farther when you're in Ohio. The cost of housing is one the best deals you will find because it is 15 percent lower than other U.S. states.

Cincinnati has the lowest overall cost of living, ranking the lowest in the categories of groceries, housing and miscellaneous goods and services (e.g., dry cleaning). Cleveland is the next cheapest place to live. It has the lowest transportation and health care. While coming in last in this three-horse race, Columbus has plenty to brag about—it still is under the national average in miscellaneous goods and services, transportation and groceries.

THE ENTREPRENEURIAL SPIRIT

Greetings from Ohio

Ohio is home to three greeting card companies: Gibson Greeting, Inc., American Greetings and the Amberley Greeting Card Company. Gibson Greeting Inc. of Cincinnati is the oldest of the bunch, having been founded in 1850. American Greetings got its start in Cleveland in 1906 and Amberley, also in Cincinnati, is the youngest of the group, opening its doors for business in 1966.

The Ohio Art Company

In the tiny town of Archbold, Ohio, a dentist by the name of Henry Winzeler decided to leave his practice in order to sell oval picture frames. The year was 1900 and even back then that was considered a dramatic career change. He borrowed money to start his picture frame business, sold his dentistry practice and bought a grocery store, using its profits to fund his first business.

In 1908, Winzeler officially launched The Ohio Art Company. The company didn't include toys until the advent of the First World War. Toy imports were interrupted, giving domestic toymakers a void in the market just waiting for them to fill. From 1914, The Ohio Art Company found a profitable niche in the toy industry and began to branch out and acquire different companies, both toy and non-toy. However, it would be a discovery at a European toy show that would forever link its identity toys. The "Etch A Sketch" was invented by Arthur Granjean of France, who called it "L'écran Magique" (The Magic Crayon). The Ohio Art Company bought it in 1959, renamed it and brought it to the public in time for the 1960 holiday season. The toy was a huge hit and remains the flagship toy of The Ohio Art Company to this day.

From Civil War to Swing

Randolph Wurlizter opened his musical instrument factory in 1861 and supplied the government as well as the general public with drums and trumpets. When the Great Depression slashed his sales in the late 1930s, the company thought outside the box and came up with the Wurlitzer Simplex, a jukebox famous during the Big Band and Swing era.

Limited by Namesake Only

"Think small. Do business one customer at a time and focus on their needs." It was with those words that Dayton native Les Wexner grew his business, Limited Brands, from his kitchen into the billion dollar conglomerate that it is today. Victoria's Secret, Express, Lane Bryant and Lerner New York and Abercrombie and Fitch are only a part of the business portfolio. Known as the richest man in Ohio, Wexner is also known as a generous philanthropist.

Nationwide Coverage

It all began when farmers complained that they were being charged urban rates for rural insurance. In December 1925, the Ohio Farm Bureau Federation responded by incorporating the Farm Bureau Mutual Automobile Insurance Company in Columbus. The company quickly grew, opened branches in other states and began to write policies for more than just cars. Farm Bureau Mutual changed its name to Nationwide Insurance in 1955 to reflect its impressive growth. The company is now one of the largest insurance and financial services companies in the world, focusing on domestic property and casualty insurance, life insurance and retirement savings, asset management and strategic investments.

Wendy's International

Known for the red-haired girl with pigtails in its logo, Wendy's International grew from one restaurant in 1969 in Columbus to an international fast food chain with more than 6300 restaurants in North America and 300 worldwide.

Founded by Dave Thomas, the restaurant was named after his eight-year old daughter Melinda Lou, who was called "Wendy" by her siblings. With simple menus and higher quality ingredients than normally used in fast food chains, Wendy's Old Fashioned Hamburgers was a huge success. In conjunction with an offbeat advertising campaign (known especially for the "Where's the Beef" commercial with senior citizen Clara Pellar), Wendy's became a household name. Wendy's International bought Canada's second-largest restaurant chain, Tim Horton's, in 1995. Tim Horton's menu offers complimentary products in comparison to Wendy's; it specializes in soups, fresh-baked goods and home-style sandwiches.

The phrase "Where's the Beef?" became so popular that Walter Mondale used it in his 1984 presidential campaign to lampoon opponent Gary Hart.

Chef Boyardee

In 1926, Cleveland fell in love with a spaghetti sauce that was being made in a restaurant called Il Giardino d'Italia. Patrons would ask for extra helpings with their meal and then requested even more afterwards, so the restaurant obliged by filling up old milk bottles with the tasty sauce so they could take it home. The genius behind the sauce? A short order cook by the name of Hector Boiardi, who also happened to be the owner of the restaurant.

Demand for his sauce grew so much that he constructed a tiny factory to keep up with the orders. Realizing his product might appeal to a bigger market, he successfully marketed the sauce (now with pasta), and proud of Italian heritage, he made sure the labels had the phonetic spelling of his last name so customers could correctly pronounce it.

At the time of his death at the age of 87, Chef Boyardee's company brought in $500 million in revenue. Not bad for an immigrant Italian kid from Cleveland.

The J. M. Smucker Company

Founded in 1897 in the small town of Orrville, Jerome Monroe Smucker began making apple cider and apple butter from his mill. His recipes must have been something special because it wasn't long before his products were in continuous demand in the region and, eventually, throughout the country. Known for its line of fruit spreads and peanut butter, the company is still run by the Smucker family.

 J.M. Smucker used apples from trees that were planted by Johnny Appleseed.

Huffy Corporation

Following in the legacy of the Wright Brothers, the Huffy Corporation was founded in Dayton in 1924. Known as the Huffman Manufacturing Corporation back then, the company specialized in making service station equipment. Founder Horace Huffman turned to making bicycles in 1934 to offer a cheaper form of transportation during the Great Depression. Success followed and the Huffy Corporation is now the largest manufacturer of bicycles in the world.

Home of the Sliders

Known as America's oldest fast food chain, White Castle has called Columbus home since 1933. The restaurant is famous for its hamburgers that don't look like your normal, everyday hamburgers. White Castle cooks small, square hamburgers that have five holes and are served in a "hamburger holder" box. Often referred to as "sliders" for their propensity to travel the human gastrointestinal tract rather quickly, these hamburgers have created legions of loyal fans from Minnesota to New Jersey to Tennessee.

White Castle is known for many firsts in the fast food industry: first hamburger chain, first industrial-strength spatula, first mass-produced paper hat, first to sell a million, then a billion, hamburgers and, finally, the first to sell frozen fast food in grocery stores.

White Castle has been referenced to or shown in five major films, most notably *Saturday Night Fever* and most recently, *Harold and Kumar Go to White Castle*.

Proctor and Gamble

A candle maker. A soap maker. Brother-in-laws. And the founding of a company on Halloween. It sounds like an unlikely start to the number one maker of household products in the world, but William Proctor and James Gamble proved otherwise.

Proctor had emigrated from England after losing his shop to fire; Gamble arrived in 1819 with his family from a famine-stricken Ireland. Both settled in Cincinnati and became acquainted with each other when they realized they were courting sisters. At the suggestion of their future father-in-law, they combined their business interests to create their own company in 1837.

Although the business was successful with its candle sales, it would be an accident with a soap product that would take it to the front of the business pack. In 1878, Proctor and Gamble had introduced a product called "White Soap" to the market. During production one day, a worker accidentally left the soap mixer on while eating his lunch, creating more air in the final product than intended. Shortly afterwards, the company began receiving orders for their "floating soap," which bewildered Proctor and Gamble. A few inquiries later, the situation was cleared up and P & G, recognizing the value in the mistake, changed the recipe permanently to insure the soap's buoyancy. It would be William Proctor's son Harley who would later change the name to "Ivory Soap." The sales of the soap would propel the company to national proportions to become the world's leader in beauty, health and household care products.

TRANSPORTATION

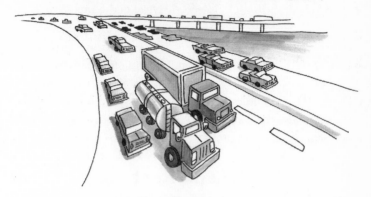

On the Road

Ohio is within 600 miles of 60 percent of the population of the United States and 50 percent of the population of Canada. The state is centrally located for business as well: 63 percent of U.S. manufacturing facilities and 80 percent of U.S. business headquarters are within a day's drive. As a result, there are several well-developed interstate highways and lesser, but no less important, roadways.

In 2006, Ohio had the 7th largest highway system as well as the 4th largest interstate system in the nation. Good thing, too, because the state had the 5th largest volume of traffic and the 3rd greatest value of truck freight.

Major East-West corridors:

☛ The Ohio Turnpike (I-80/I-90)

☛ I-76 from Akron to Pennsylvania

☛ U.S. 30 through Canton, Mansfield and Lima

☛ I-70 through Columbus and Dayton

☛ The Appalachian Highway (State Route 32)

Major North-South corridors:

☛ I-75 running through Toledo, Dayton and Cincinnati

☛ I-71 from Cleveland to Columbus and Cincinnati

☛ I-77 from Cleveland to Akron, Canton and Marietta

Ohio has 116,964 miles of public road and 1572 miles of interstate. Ohio also has 228 miles of the historic National Road, the first major federal road project.

Hit the Road

In 2005, approximately 83 percent of Ohio's commuters drove to work alone; 8 percent carpooled; 2 percent used public transportation; another 2 percent walked; 0.8 percent used other means; and another 2 percent had the most pleasant commute of all—they walked from their bedroom to their home office.

DID YOU KNOW?

The Ohio Department of Transportation maintains over 3100 miles of guardrail.

Fly the Sky

Ohio has six primary and commercial service airports and 94 general aviation airports. Port Columbus International Airport served 6,611,575 passengers in 2005; Dayton International Airport boarded 1,122,243 people onto planes; and the Cincinnati/Northern Kentucky International Airport served a staggering 22 million passengers in 2005. The two states share the airport; Cincinnati needed to build an airport and Kentucky, just a few hundred feet across the river, was happy to provide the space.

GENERAL HEALTH AND WELLNESS

Life Expectancy

Ohio ranked 36th for life expectancy according to a 2006 report published by the peer-reviewed medical journal *PLoS* (*Public Library of Science*) *Medicine*. Based on 2000 figures, the average life expectancy in Ohio is 76.4 years. Women generally live longer, with a life expectancy of about 78.7 years and Ohio men can expect to make it to 73.8 years. In comparison, Hawaii is first on the list for longevity, with an average life expectancy of 80 years, while Mississippi brought up the rear at an average of 73.6 years.

The "h" in Ohio is for "heavy"

Ohio residents have a tendency to take on the same shape as their state's name: round on both ends. Obesity rates in Ohio make it 13th heaviest state in the nation, a trend that is both troubling and expensive. Why is Ohio like that? Reasons vary, but the most likely causes include a lack of walker-friendly architectural designs in suburban neighborhoods, uncooperative weather conditions through more than a third of the year and, last but not least, a love of food that's as big as the state itself.

Trying To Pull Rank

The United Health Foundation, a not-for-profit private foundation, in partnership with the American Public Health Association and Partnership for Prevention, produces a yearly report that assesses the health of the nation based on determinants such as personal behaviors, community environment, availability of affordable health insurance, the quality of medical care from health professionals, as well as other factors. When analyzed,

these factors give a snapshot view of each state's overall health—
a kind of yearly checkup, so to speak.

The 2006 report ranks Ohio as 25th in the nation for health;
an improvement from 27th place it held last year. What
improved? Smoking decreased by 14 percent and immunization
coverage increased by 6 percent. Ohio showed strengths in areas
that contributed to the better ranking, such as a low rate of
motor vehicle deaths (1.2 deaths per 100,000,000 miles driven)
and a high percentage of pregnant women receiving proper pre-
natal care (over 80 percent).

The state still faces a handful of major challenges in its quest to
become healthier. The smoking rate is still high (22% of the
population still smokes); a high rate of cancer deaths (214 per
100,000) and a high rate of deaths from cardiovascular disease
(343 per 100,000). On a comforting note, 15 of Ohio's hospitals made the 2006 "Best Hospitals List" from *U.S. News &
World Report.*

OLDEST SCHOOLS

"No matter where you are in Ohio, you are never more than 30 minutes to the nearest university or college."

–Ohio saying

Schoenbrunn

The first school in Ohio was in business even before Ohio was a state—and it wasn't even for the settlers! Located near present day New Philadelphia, the village of Schoenbrunn established a school in 1772 that taught Native Americans reading and writing. Run by Moravian Missionaries, this school was a successful and unique cultural example of European and Native American co-existence until it was forced to close in 1777 because of the American Revolution.

Ohio University

In 1804, the state legislature chartered Ohio University in Athens, making it the oldest university in the Northwest Territory. Modeled after Yale University's charter, Ohio University opened as an academy in 1808 with three students and awarded its first bachelor degrees in 1815. The university graduated a total of 145 students in the years leading up to the Civil War. Today, the university teaches over 19,000 students and is designated a Doctoral/Research-Extensive university by the Carnegie Foundation for the Advancement of Teaching.

An interesting historical note from Ohio University: William Holmes McGuffey, president of the university from 1839 to 1843, was also the originator of the venerable series, McGuffey's Eclectic Readers. Responsible for education several generations of Americans, the Readers were the most successful first readers ever produced, selling over 120 million copies.

DID YOU KNOW?

Athens County's "Coonskin Library" started distributing books in 1804. Incorporated as the Western Library Association in 1810, subscribers were fined if they got fingerprints on the pages of the books.

Kenyon College

Ohio's oldest private college got its start in 1824 when Bishop Philander Chase, appalled at the lack of trained clergy in the Ohio frontier area, solicited funds and land from Lord Gambier and Lord Kenyon in England to create a seminary. Kenyon College's alumni list showcases several recognizable names, including President Rutherford B. Hayes, actors Paul Newman and Jonathon Winters, former Secretary of the Treasury John W. Snow and CNN anchor Kris Osborn.

The first free public school system was established in Cincinnati in 1825.

HIGHER LEARNING

Education Forever

"...Schools and the means of education shall forever be encouraged," so says the Northwest Ordinance of 1787, the territory from which Ohio was carved. With a total of 145 public and private institutions of higher learning within the boundaries of the state, one is tempted to say that Ohioans took the phrase from the ordinance pretty seriously.

The state of Ohio has:

☛ 13 state universities

☛ 24 state university branch and regional campuses

☛ 46 liberal arts colleges and universities

☛ 6 state assisted medical schools

☛ 2 private medical schools

☛ 15 community colleges

☛ 8 technical colleges

☛ Over 24 independent non-profit colleges

Of those higher institutions, *U.S. News and World Report* ranked Ohio State University in the top 60 of the nation's best universities, Ohio Wesleyan University in the top 100 of the nation's best liberal arts colleges and Ohio Northern University in the top 10 best comprehensive colleges in the nation. Case Western Reserve University earned the prestigious honor of being ranked in the top 60 best universities in the world.

To fill all those classroom seats, Ohio has more than 457,000 college students.

TRENDS IN EDUCATION

Who's Going to School?

While the state has plenty of schools to pick from, the surrounding population doesn't seem to be too interested in choosing. When compared to other states, Ohio ranks 40th in the number of people with associate degrees and 41st in the number of bachelor degrees earned.

Average Student-Teacher Ratio

Ohio ranks 28th in the nation for student-teacher ratios, with an average of 15.2 students per teacher.

Literacy

Ohio's ACT and SAT scores are higher than the national average. Students scored an average of 54 points higher on the SAT and, not as dramatically, 1 to 2 points higher on the ACT test.

Cincinnati is currently the 9th most literate city in the nation, with Columbus not far behind at 12th and Cleveland ranking 18th. Ohio has earned kudos for its libraries, as well. In a 2006 study by Thomas J. Hennen, Ohio ranked 1st in a state-by-state comparison and its three biggest library systems were ranked in the nation's top 10 for cities of 500,000 or more.

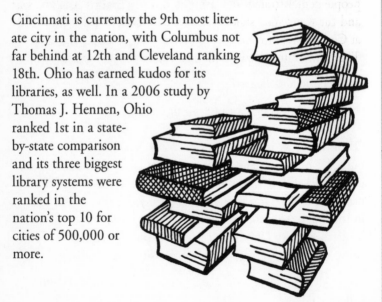

NOTABLE EVENTS

Student Revolution

The Kent State shootings rocked the nation and became a defining moment in America's socially turbulent decade. On May 4th, 1970, 77 National Guardsmen began clearing an already planned protest. Students began confronting them, some throwing rocks and volleying back the tear gas canisters that the guardsmen had thrown into the crowd. When some of the students began coming forward slowly towards the guardsmen, 29 of them opened fire, killing four students and injuring nine. Two of the killed were not protestors; they were students walking from one class to another.

The national response to the shootings was dramatic. Hundreds of universities, colleges, high schools and even elementary schools closed throughout the United States because of a student strike of eight million students. Five days after the shooting, 100,000 people demonstrated in Washington, D.C. against both the war and the Kent State shootings. President Nixon was sequestered at Camp David for his own protection for the next two days. The Kent State campus remained closed for six weeks.

VOTING TRENDS

Swing State

When it comes to cold reality of politics, Ohio is one hot state. Because of its diverse make up of blue and white collar work forces and its blend of rural and urban populations, the state also has a good mixture of Republican and Democratic areas. Because of this demographic mix, Ohio is considered by many to be a microcosm of the nation—a Republican presidential candidate has never won the White House without winning Ohio. Since 1892, with the exception of two races, Ohio has always gone to the winner of the elections. In addition, it has 20 electoral votes, more than most swing states, so it can influence the outcome of an election based on that alone.

The Democratic side of the state is in the northeast, where industry dominates. East from Cleveland to the state border and south down to Mahoning county encompasses the majority of the Democratic territory. Southwestern Ohio is where Republicans tend to congregate. Cincinnati and the surrounding areas are particularly partial to the party.

Ohio was a deciding state in three elections:

☛ In 2004: George W. Bush just barely won Ohio's electoral votes, by a slim margin of 2 percent over John Kerry

☛ In 1976: Democrat Jimmy Carter defeated Republican Gerald Ford with just 0.2 percent more votes.

☛ In 1948: Democrat President Harry S. Truman triumphed over Republican Dewey Thomas by slipping by him with just 1 percent more votes, considered the greatest election upset in American history.

Mother of Presidents

Seven presidents were born in Ohio, and an eighth president adopted the state as his own, making Ohio the home of 8 U.S. presidents and earning it the above title. As for the adopted one, William Henry Harrison was born in Virginia but settled on a farm in North Bend, Ohio and was living there when he was elected president. All but one of the presidents was Republican, except for Harrison.

The eight presidents are:

☛ William Henry Harrison (1773–1841), 9th president

☛ Ulysses S. Simpson Grant (1822–85), 18th president

☛ Rutherford Birchard Hayes (1822–93), 19th president

☛ James Abram Garfield (1831–81), 20th president

☛ Benjamin Harrison (1833–1901), 23rd president

☛ William McKinley (1843–1901), 25th president

☛ William Howard Taft (1857–1930), 27th president

☛ Warren Gamaliel Harding (1865–1923), 29th president

A State with Influence

Ohio was the dominant state in politics for 70 years, from the Civil War to Harding's term in 1920. Historians attribute it to Ohio's broad constituency, which force any successful political figure to reconcile major differences among the people. Because of its microcosm environment, Ohio became a training ground for national leaders.

DID YOU  **KNOW?**

Rutherford B. Hayes was the first president to take the oath of office in the White House.

NOTABLE FIGURES IN OHIO POLITICS

Donna Shalala (b. 1941)

Born in Cleveland in 1941, Shalala was appointed United States Secretary of Health and Human Services in 1993 by President Clinton. She became the nation's longest serving HHS Secretary, staying in her position for eight years.

James M. Cox (1870–1957)

First a reporter, then the owner of the *Dayton News* and the *Dayton Daily News* as well as several other papers, Cox moved from newspaper editor and owner to U.S. representative in 1909. Born in Jackson, he was elected governor of Ohio twice and in 1920 was nominated as a presidential candidate by the Democratic Party with Franklin Delano Roosevelt as his running mate. He was defeated by another Ohioan, Warren G. Harding.

William Saxbe (b. 1916)

Born into the farming community of Mechanicsburg, this son of a cattle buyer became U. S. Senator as well as U.S. Attorney General for presidents Nixon and Ford. He also served as ambassador to India under Ford's term.

Outspoken and pragmatic, Saxbe ruffled political feathers—including President Nixon's, earning him a two-year ban from the president's office—with his views on the Vietnam War as well as the business of politics in Congress. Frustrated with the slow pace of legislation, he partnered with Senator Alan M. Cranston to create a two-track system for the movement of legislation through the Senate.

Saxbe served in the Senate until 1974, when he was appointed U.S. Attorney General; he remained in the position until 1975. Appointed ambassador to India, he attended to his duties until 1977 when he retired to practice law in Mechanicsburg.

Kennesaw Mountain Landis (1866-1944)

Known for making tough but fair decisions, Landis came from the tiny town of Millville in Butler county and would earn his law degree from Northwestern University Law School. He served as a U.S. district judge in Illinois. In 1920 he was appointed to the post of baseball commissioner to deal with the aftermath of the 1919 "Black Sox" scandal. Landis barred the eight Chicago White Sox players from organized baseball, and further strict measures employed by him in the game raised the ideal of baseball back out of the gutter and into the welcoming arms of the American public.

Robert Alphonso "Bob" Taft (b. 1942)

Although popular enough to be elected to a second term, the great grandson of President William Howard Taft became Ohio's first governor to be convicted on criminal charges by failing to disclose $6,000 worth of golf outings and gifts from businessmen and lobbyists (state office holders are required by law to report any gifts valued at over $75). He received a public reprimand from the Ohio Supreme Court and was ordered to pay a $4,000 fine as well as write an apology to all Ohioans.

RUNNING ON THE RAILS OF POLITICS

The Underground Railroad to Freedom

Legend has it that in 1831 a runaway slave named Tice Davids slipped into the Ohio River while trying to shake off his hot-on-his-heels owner. Tice swam for his life across the river while the other man sought out a boat to row after him. Tice landed first in Ripley, Ohio and immediately disappeared from view. The owner continued to search for Tice, but eventually gave up. In frustration, the man concluded that it was as though Tice had "gone off on an underground railroad..."

With the abolishment of slavery in the Northwest Ordinance of 1787, Ohio was a state that became a pivotal point for thousands of slaves fleeing up from the South and toward Canada. Amazingly well organized at a time of primitive covert operations and no mass communication, Ohio had over 3000 miles of escape routes that traversed forests, towns and farms.

Generally speaking, most of the routes pointed in a northerly direction. Along the Ohio River, no less than 23 entry points were established for relatively safe crossing. Even with the extraordinary number of entrances and pathways, traveling the Underground Railroad was dangerous, difficult and often deadly. Even though Ohio was a free state, federal laws still allowed for legal capture of slaves in free territory. Any person who was caught harboring, aiding or concealing a fugitive was subject to a $500 fine. Those who hindered the arrest of such slaves were also fined. Spurred by successful transfers of slaves, The Fugitive Slave Law of 1850 raised the risk exponentially by levying fines of $1000 along with prison sentences to those who helped the slaves. It also mandated citizens to help federal marshals when called upon in the capture of slaves. In addition, bounty hunters who sought runaway slaves didn't take time to differentiate between escaped and free ones.

Despite these heavy punishments and dangers, Ohioans kept the Railroad running by using secret signals, veiled language terms and songs. The people who helped slaves escape were "conductors." Safe places like houses or barns were "stations" and the person in charge of the stations were the "station masters." Depending on the situation, escaped slaves still traveling were called either passengers or baggage. It was an extraordinary effort made by hundreds of individuals for more than 50 years to ensure the safe passage of slaves. While accurate numbers are hard to come by, it is estimated that at least 40,000 people pass through Ohio from 1816 to the end of the Civil War in 1865.

FRIENDLY FOREIGN RELATIONS

You're from Ohio, Eh?

The United States and Canada share over 4000 miles of borders and together they share the title of having the world's longest undefended border in the world. With its close proximity to Canada (Pelee Island in Lake Erie is the southernmost point of Canada, just a few miles away from the Ohio border), the state of Ohio has also strived to maintain a good working relationship with its northern neighbor. The Ohio-Canada relationship benefits both parties in the forms of trade and tourism.

Here's a snapshot of the trade picture:

- In 2005, Canada was Ohio's largest and most valuable export market with trade between the partners almost equivalent to Ohio's export sales to all other countries combined. In dollar terms, this means nearly $17 billion in export sales for Ohio.

- Ohio's leading exports to Canada were motor vehicle parts, automobiles, motor vehicle engines and trucks. Oddly enough, Ohio also exports air conditioning and refrigeration equipment up north as well.

- Ohio's imports from Canada topped $13.7 billion, with crude petroleum and motor vehicle parts leading the way in dollars exchanged.

- Ohio also relies on Canada for aluminum, steel products, newsprint, lumber and plastics.

- The Ohio-Canada tourism business is booming. Ohio residents made 698,400 visits to Canada in 2005, spending $235 million. Canadians made more than 511,300 visits to Ohio, spending $96 million.

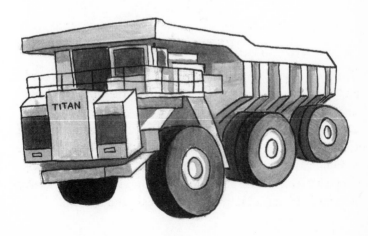

But Wait, There's More...

Ohio and Canada have forged a few unique partnerships for different reasons, although all of them are good!

The Canada-United States Law Institute is a bi-national, non-profit, multi-disciplinary establishment created in 1976 by Case Western Reserve University School of Law of Cleveland and the Faculty of Law at the University of Western Ontario. The Institute cultivates student and faculty exchanges, develops Canada-U.S. scholarships, publishes a bi-national law journal and sponsors an annual conference focusing on bi-national legal and policy issues.

Located in Cincinnati and operating out of facilities that total more than 117,000 square feet, Heroux-Devtek of Quebec specializes in the design, development, manufacture and repair of aerospace and industrial products.

ENVIRONMENTAL ISSUES

Clean Coal

The Canadian Clean Power Coalition and the Ohio Coal Research Center at Ohio University are finding ways to reduce greenhouse emission from coal-fired electricity— generating plants by collaborating on "clean coal" initiatives. Some of the initiatives include using current reduction technologies like scrubbers, sharing of best practices and collaboration on other technologies. American Electric Power, based in Columbus, Ohio, will build one or more advance technology power plants in the company's eastern service area in the next few years.

THE STARS BURN BRIGHTLY IN OHIO

Halle Berry

Named after a local department store, Halle Berry was born in 1966 and was raised in her hometown of Cleveland. After entering several beauty contests, including Miss Ohio (first runner up) and Miss World in 1986 (sixth place), in 1988 she auditioned for a role in the updated version of Aaron Spelling's television series *Charlie's Angels*. Although she did not land a part, Spelling encouraged her to continue acting. She followed his advice and eventually became the first African American woman to win the Academy Award for Best Actress, in 2001.

Clark Gable

An Academy Award-winning actor and mega film star during the 1930s and 1940s, Clark Gable was born in 1901 as William Clark Gable in the small town of Cadiz, Ohio. Best known for his role as Rhett Butler in the movie *Gone With the Wind*, he joined the U.S. Army Air Forces in 1942 and was bestowed with the dubious honor of having a bounty put on his head by Adolph Hitler.

The four Warner brothers of the enormous production company Warner Brothers Entertainment, Inc. began their careers in 1903 by showing films on their own movie projector to coal miners in Ohio.

Drew Carey

Funny man and actor Drew Carey was born in Cleveland in 1958. After serving a stint in the U.S. Marine Corps reserve, Drew struggled to make it as a stand-up comic and worked as a bank teller and waiter during the 1980s to support himself. Drew's career finally hit the big time after his first appearance on *The Tonight Show* starring Johnny Carson in 1991. His popularity became permanently cemented after starring in his self-titled television show, *The Drew Carey Show*, and hosting the U.S. version of *Whose Line Is It Anyway?*

DID YOU KNOW?

Cleveland native Margaret Hamilton, the green-faced wicked witch in *The Wizard of Oz*, was a manager of a nursery school.

Dean Martin

Speaking only Italian until the age of five, Dean Martin was born in 1917 in Steubenville, close to the eastern Ohio border. He dropped out of school in the tenth grade and became a whiskey runner, a boxer and a steel mill worker. It was only after working in an illegal casino that he decided to try singing as a way to make money. He went on to become one of the most famous music artists from the 1950s and 1960s—even topping the Beatles—as well as being known for his film acting and television work.

Paul Newman

Born in 1925 near Cleveland, acting great Paul Newman is still
hailed as a major influence for younger actors today. He first
appeared on the silver screen in 1954 and hasn't stopped since
then. This Academy Award-, Golden Globe- and Emmy Award-
winning actor is also known as a professional auto racing driver,
philanthropist, author, founder of a rehabilitation center for
drug abusers and the owner of his own food company,
Newman's Own.

DID YOU  KNOW?

Fans of the long running television series *M*A*S*H** can see
memorabilia from the set in Tony Packo's Café located in
Toledo. Jamie Farr (Max Klinger) is a Toledo native and mentioned Tony Packo's in the series several times.

Sarah Jessica Parker
Fame placed its permanent laurels on Sarah Jessica Parker when
she played character Carrie Bradshaw in the very popular HBO
television series *Sex and the City*. Born in Nelsonville in 1965,
she and her family moved to Cincinnati where she began training as an actress and ballet dancer. Her family moved again
a few years later to just outside New York City where Sarah
quickly started landing theater and television roles. She eventually earned an Emmy and a Golden Globe for her work and
continues to act in theater, on television and on the big screen.

Bob Hope
Originally born in England as Leslie Townes Hope, Bob Hope
moved to Cleveland in 1908 at the age of five. Comedian,
vaudevillian, singer, actor and dancer, Bob Hope started his
career when he was just 12 and has performed in almost every
type of entertainment venue since then. Famed for his skill with
one-liners as well his ultimate comedic timing, Bob Hope

received numerous awards, performed for 11 U.S. presidents and was voted among the best top 50 comedy acts ever by fellow comedians and comedy insiders in a 2005 poll. He lived to the age of 100 and when asked a few months before his death where he would like to be buried, he is quoted as saying "Surprise me."

 Don't have a cow, man! The voice of Bart Simpson, of the animated show *The Simpsons*, is Nancy Cartwright of Kettering (near Dayton).

A Partial List of Notable Movies Made in Ohio

Air Force One
Antwone Fisher
The Deerhunter
Brubaker
A Christmas Story
Gung Ho
Eight Men Out
Plains, Trains and Automobiles
Rain Man
Major League
Tango and Cash
Little Man Tate
A Rage in Harlem
The Shawshank Redemption
Spider Man 3

DID YOU KNOW?

Superstar director Steven Spielberg is from Ohio. He was born in Cincinnati in 1947.

AND THE BEAT GOES ON...

Chrissie Hynde

Born in 1951 in Akron, Chrissie Ellen Hynde grew up to become a rarity in the 1970s and 1980s world of rock and roll: a successful female band leader. Her steadfast determination to be true to herself as well as her music garnered her respect from all quarters of the music industry. She became a role model for younger girls and even influenced punk and new wave fashions—reportedly giving Sid Vicious of the Sex Pistols his trademark lock necklace. Although her band members have come and gone, Chrissie Hynde remains the anchor of the group and continues to write, perform and produce music today.

James Ingram

Another musician from Akron, James Ingram was born in 1956. Self-taught, James is known for his soul vocal performance as well as for his talent in producing and songwriting. He also plays several instruments and owns his own record label. He has performed with or written for such musical greats as Ray Charles, Linda Ronstadt, Michael McDonald, Natalie Cole, Kenny Rogers and Michael Jackson.

Devo

Akron must have something in the water, because the rock group called Devo was formed there, too, in 1972. The Mothersbaugh brothers, Mark and Bob, and the Casale brothers, Gerald and Bob, would eventually form the quartet foundation of the group, with other members coming and going on a rather fluid basis. Best know for their hit "Whip It" which went to #14 on Billboard's Hot 100 in 1980, they were on the cutting edge of several 1980s music phenomena: music videos, synthesizer instrumentation and the tongue-in-cheek cultural satire that weaved itself through their fashions, lyrics and performances.

Nick Lachey

Perhaps the most well-known member of the popular boy band 98 Degrees, Nick Lachey was born on the Kentucky-Virginia border in 1973, but grew up in Cincinnati. This singer and song writer became a permanent fixture in the public's eye after starring with his then-wife Jessica Simpson in the MTV reality series *Newlyweds*. He has won awards for his song and music video "What's Left of Me" and was nominated Favorite Male Pop/Rock Artist in 2006.

Marilyn Manson

Born as Brian Hugh Warner in 1969 in Canton, Marilyn Manson would grow up to become the leader of one of the most widely known "shock rock" bands in the U.S. during the 1990s. This self-dubbed "Antichrist Superstar" singer combined masterful marketing techniques, controversial and often taboo subject matter with theatrical elements to transform a generation of apathetic white suburban teens into cult-like followers. He has numerous acting credits for both television and movies roles, is known for his talent in watercolor painting and is also an honorary member of the Church of Satan.

Henry Mancini

Born in 1924, under the very Italian name of Enrico Nicola
Mancini, Henry Mancini is one of Cleveland's own. Growing
up with a father who was an avid flutist, he attended the Julliard
School of Music in New York City but was drafted for service
in World War II before finishing his studies. In 1946, he began
composing professionally and throughout his career he would
be nominated for an unprecedented 72 Grammies, 20 of which
he would win. He also won four Academy Awards, one Golden
Globe and would be nominated for two Emmys. Best remembered for the *Pink Panther* theme, he is credited with helping to
bring jazz into movie and television scores.

Pere Ubu

Cited as "the world's only expressionist rock 'n' roll band," the
rock music group called Pere Ubu was formed in Cleveland in
1975 and has influenced musicians all around the globe since
then. Named after the protagonist in the surrealist play *Ubu
Roi*, the band's style combines experimental music, bluesy
garage rock and a healthy dose of punk. While never reaching
mass popularity as a mainstream band, Pere Ubu is nevertheless
a critically acclaimed group whose artistry and unique take on
music continues to inspire generations of avant-garde musicians.

Bow Wow
Rapper and actor Bow Wow was born in Columbus in 1987.
Christened Shad Gregory Moss, Bow Wow received his canine
nickname at age six from rapper Snoop Dogg and Dr. Dre after
they saw him perform onstage. Known as Lil' Bow Wow then,
he officially went to work as Dr. Dre's opening act and also
appeared on television with Snoop. At age 13, he released his
first album, which went platinum twice. He has since released
four more albums, each reaching either platinum or gold status.

He continues his screen and television acting work in addition to his music and is currently producing a cartoon for MTV, scheduled to debut in 2007.

Rascal Flatts

This contemporary country band has its roots in Columbus. Second cousins Jay Demarcus and Gary Levox, both from the state capital, founded the group more than a decade ago. Oklahoma native Joe Don Rooney joined after being invited to sit in as a substitute guitar player. Beginning in 2000, Rascal Flatts has won over 17 music awards, and their latest album *Me and My Gang* was certified quadruple platinum after only ten months on the charts.

 The first radio station in the world to play Elvis Presley music exclusively was WCVG-AM in 1988.

Benjamin Hanby

Although he was born in the summer, this composer would grow up to be remembered for snow and Santa Claus. Hanby was born near Rushville in 1833 and later moved with his family to Westerville. A United Brethren pastor with a penchant for penning hymns and songs, he became famous for his anti-slavery tune "Darling Nelly Gray." At the height of the song's popularity, Hanby wrote to the Boston music publisher about his royalties and they replied that his popularity was payment enough—he never received any money. Hanby would later write another song that remains popular to this day: the Christmas carol "Up on the Housetop." Chicago Publisher Root and Cady bought the song in 1864, but Hanby would not live to see many royalty checks. He died of tuberculosis in 1867.

THE PRINTED PAGE

Erma Bombeck

American humorist Erma Bombeck was born in Dayton in 1927. She found fame through her newspaper columns, which chronicled the everyday life of a housewife. Debuting in 1964, she became syndicated in 1965 and eventually published more than 4000 columns. She authored 13 best-selling books and had a television sitcom called *Maggie* based on her self-deprecating comedy. Not too bad for a woman who was once told by a college guidance counselor that she would never be a successful writer.

James Thurber

Born in Columbus in 1894, James Thurber became well-known for both his writing as well as his drawings for *New Yorker* magazine. His humorous short stories have been turned into Broadway productions and movies; a network television show based on his writings and his life ran from 1969 to 1970. In 1997, the Thurber Prize was established to honor outstanding examples of humor.

R.L. Stine

Likened to Stephen King for kids, author R.L. Stine was born in 1943 in Columbus. He graduated from Ohio State University with a degree in English and began writing books for children and teenagers. His supernatural thriller series for middle graders called Goosebumps became a huge success and was turned into a television series. Stine has also written several other books dealing with otherworldly subjects and has penned several humor books as well.

Harriet Beecher Stowe

Born in Litchfield, Connecticut in 1811, Harriet Beecher Stowe moved to Cincinnati in 1832. Cincinnati was one of many hubs for the abolitionist movement, and it was there that she was inspired to write *Uncle Tom's Cabin*, the novel that had an enormous impact on how African Americans and the slave trade were viewed, both in the United States and Europe. The brutal and cruel reality of slavery depicted in her book had a polarizing effect on both the northern and southern states and was even blamed for fanning the emotional fires that fueled the Civil War. So large was the book's influence that Abraham Lincoln remarked upon meeting her, "So this is the little lady who made this big war."

Toni Morrison

Nobel and Pulitzer Prize-winning author Toni Morrison was born under the name of Chloe Anthony Wofford in Lorain in 1931. Her first two novels *The Bluest Eye* (winner of the Pulitzer Prize) and *Sula* were based in Ohio. She was awarded the Nobel Prize for Literature in 1993 for her six novels—the first African American to receive the award. She recently retired from her position as a Professor of Humanities at Princeton.

Paul Laurence Dunbar

Born in Dayton in 1872, poet Paul Laurence Dunbar was the son of former slaves. He showed an early talent for words—he wrote his first poem when he was six years old and gave his first public poetry recital just three years later. He would later win worldwide acclaim and popularity with his poetry, novels, short stories, song lyrics and plays, touring both America and Europe to packed auditoriums. His untimely death at age 33 from tuberculosis cut short his brilliant career.

DID YOU 🏠 KNOW?

Two good friends of Paul Laurence Dunbar convinced him to publish his first poem in high school. They were none other than Wilbur Wright and Orville Wright, the pioneers of aviation.

Zane Grey

One of the first authors ever to make millions through his writing, Zane Grey brought the Wild West to readers through his 90 novels. Born Pearl Zane Grey in Zanesville in 1872, he dropped his first name as an adult while playing minor league baseball and sporadically practicing dentistry, for which he had gone to school. His fascination with the West began in 1907 after hunting mountain lions in Arizona. Drawing on the legend of his great-great-great aunt, a revolutionary war heroine, his first book, *Betty Zane*, memorialized her. Published in 1910, it became a bestseller, beginning a prolific career that continued until his death in 1932.

Gloria Steinem

Forever associated with the feminist movement, Gloria Marie Steinem was born in Toledo in 1934. Frustrated by the male-dominated environment in the workplace, she lobbied for equal rights for women when she wrote an article for *Esquire* magazine in 1962 criticizing the fact that women were forced to choose either marriage or a stunted career upon entry into adulthood. Steinem went on to co-found two organizations: the National Women's Political Caucus and the Women's Action Alliance. She served as founding editor for the feminist magazine *MS*. She went on to found the Coalition of Labor Union Women. She was inducted into the National Women's Hall of Fame in 1993.

DID YOU  KNOW?

Contrary to popular belief, Steinem did not invent the feminist slogan "A woman needs a man like a fish needs a bicycle." It was actually said by Irina Dunn, an Australian educator, journalist and politician.

Rita Dove

Pulitzer Prize-winning U.S. Poet Laureate Rita Dove was born into a family already known for breaking barriers. Her father was the first African American research chemist who broke through the racial barrier in the tire industry. Born in 1952, Rita would grow up to be remarkably talented and gifted. She graduated from high school as a Presidential Scholar (one of the top 100 American high school graduates in the nation) and would then graduate summa cum laude from Miami University in Oxford, Ohio. She received the Pulitzer Prize in 1987 for her poetry collection *Thomas and Beulah*, poems loosely based on her maternal grandparents. In 1993, she was appointed Poet Laureate of the United States and Consultant in Poetry at the Library of Congress, making her the first African American, as well as the youngest person ever to receive the appointment. She has gone on to win numerous awards and accolades for her poetry and currently is the Commonwealth Professor of English as well as Chair at the University of Virginia at Charlottesville.

HAVE YOU HEARD THE NEWS?

Hugh Downs

This Emmy-winning news broadcaster, television show host, author and producer was born in Akron in 1921. He began his career in broadcasting at the rather young age of 18 and he would go on, according to *The Guinness Book of World Records*, to be the second person to clock the most hours in U.S. history. From announcing a children's show to announcing the news, Hugh Downs' trademark style was his low-key, professional manner. He is also an accomplished sailor, pilot and composer.

Phil Donahue

Born in Cleveland in 1935, Phil Donahue is the godfather of the TV tabloid talk show. His show, *The Phil Donahue Show*, was the longest continuously running talk show in U.S. television history, airing from 1967 to 1996. His show is credited for introducing controversial issues such as women's reproductive rights, banning prayer in schools and cross-dressing.

John Hockenberry

Born in Dayton in 1956, this NBC correspondent started his career hosting a nightly news show on National Public Radio. He has covered the Kosovo War, the Persian Gulf War and the Middle East in his career. He has also starred in an off-Broadway autobiographical production, written two books and numerous articles for the *New York Times*, the *New Yorker*, the *Washington Post*, *Wired* and many other national publications. A paraplegic since 19, he has become a role model to those who are physically-challenged.

Nina Blackwood

Born in Massachusetts in 1955 but raised in Cleveland, Nina Blackwood's signature hair and voice will forever be connected with MTV. She was the first of the five original VJs for the music video channel and has continued her association with the rock music of the 1980s through her nationally syndicated radio show, *Nina Blackwood's Absolutely 80s*. An actor as well, she has appeared in several films and television shows.

 The phrase "rock and roll" was originated by Cleveland D.J. Alan Freed.

NOTABLE PEOPLE AND EVENTS

George Bellows

George Wesley Bellows was a painter who helped bring realism to the canvas through his depictions of urban life in New York City and more importantly, the atrocities of World War I. Born in Columbus in 1882, he was a successful commercial illustrator while still in college at Ohio State University. He moved to New York City to study painting and it was there he began to gain popularity through his stylistic artwork. He also contributed to the universal acceptance of lithography as a fine art medium.

Maya Lin

While still a student in college, Maya Lin's design for the Vietnam Veteran's Memorial in Washington, D.C. was picked as the finalist. At the age of 21, she created one of the most powerful and most recognized designs in the world. Born in 1959 in Athens, Ohio, this sculptor and architect has designed the Civil Right Memorial in Montgomery, Alabama; the Groundswell Sculpture at Ohio State University; and the Input Earth sculpture at Ohio University. She has been awarded several accolades, among them the Presidential Design Award and the Architecture Prize from the American Academy of Arts and Letters. She lives in New York City and continues to design sculptures and architectural forms.

Clarence White

Born in New Carlisle in 1871, Clarence White is remembered for two things: his skill at photography and perhaps more importantly, his skill at teaching photography. Clarence showed interest in art at an early age but was encouraged to pursue more practical means of supporting himself. It was only after marrying and working as an accounting clerk that the photo bug really bit him. He pioneered the pictorial style of photograph, a type of photography that often made the picture look like a painting. He taught photography at Columbia University and eventually opened his own school of photography. He mentored some of the 20th century's greatest photographers, such as Dorothea Lange and Margaret Bourke-White.

INVENTIONS AND INNOVATIONS

A Gadget Grab Bag

Ohio is home to many inventions and innovations; some are well known, some are not; some we couldn't get through the day without and others, well, let's just say we've gotten along just fine without them.

Here is a quick round up of inventions that are distinctly Ohio:

- Artificial fish bait, Ernest Pflueger, Akron, 1883

- Automatic traffic signal, Garrett Morgan, Cleveland, 1923

- Beer can, John Leon Bennett, Newark, 1937

- Velocipede (bicycle), patented by Fisher Spofford and Matthew Raffington, Columbus, 1869

- Book matches, Ohio Columbus Barber (yes, that's his name), Barberton, 1896

- Carbonless copy paper, NCR Corporation, Dayton, 1955

- Circular life saving net, Thomas Browder, Greenfield, 1887

- Pampers (disposable diapers), Victor Mills, 1962

- Disposable vacuum cleaner bag, Robert Hallock, Columbus

- Do Little or Nothing Machine, H.B. Shriver, Savannah, 1983

- Electric dental gold annealer, Dr. Luzern Custer, Dayton, 1890

- Ethyl gasoline, Thomas Midgely, Dayton, 1920s

- Manure spreader, Joseph Oppenheim, Mercer County, 1899

☛ Mechanical corn picker, John Lambert, Ansonia, 1876

☛ Menthol cigarettes, Lloyd Hughes, Mingo Junction, 1920s

☛ Motorized spaghetti fork, William Miscavich and Paul Shutt, Canton, 1969

☛ Preparation H, Dr. Geroge Sperti, Cincinnati, 1950s

☛ Reaper, Obed Hussey, Cincinnati, 1833

☛ Refrigerator with door shelves, Powel Crosley, Jr., Cincinnati, 1932

☛ Revolving book case, Joseph Danner, Akron, 1880

☛ Self-lowering toilet seat, Gregory Janek, Connor, 1986

☛ Stepladder, John Balsley, Dayton, 1870

☛ Vacuum cleaner, Murray Spangler, Canton, 1907

THE AERIAL AGE BEGINS IN DAYTON

The Wright Brothers

While Kitty Hawk, North Carolina, may lay claim to the site of the world's first airplane flight, it's Dayton, Ohio, that has the home base advantage. It's here that the founding fathers of flight, Orville and Wilbur Wright, kept a bicycle shop that would supply the income for their real interest, aviation.

With a father who traveled frequently owing to his position as a bishop in the Church of the United Brethren of Christ, Wilbur and Orrville were born in two different states. Wilbur was born in Indiana in 1867; Orrville was born in Dayton, Ohio, in 1871. In 1878, their father came home from one of his trips with a toy helicopter for his sons. Based on an invention by French aeronautical pioneer Alphonse Penaud, the helicopter was made of paper, bamboo and cork and had a rubber band to twirl its rotor. The boys were fascinated by it and played with it until it broke, then made one for themselves. Years later when the public asked the Wright brothers what ignited their interest in aviation, they would recount the time when their father brought home that toy.

In 1889, Orville dropped out of high school to start a printing business after having built and designed his own printing press with his brother. Orrville began printing the weekly newspaper *The West Side News* and Wilbur signed on as editor to help out. Noting the bicycle craze sweeping the nation at that time, they abandoned the newspaper business and opened a bicycle repair and sales shop in 1892 and began manufacturing their own brand of bicycles in 1892. The store provided them with enough money to indulge in their interest in flight. They weren't the only ones interested in tackling the air barrier; a handful of people, most notably German glider engineer Otto Lilienthal,

Chicago engineer Octave Chanute and Smithsonian Institution Secretary Samuel Langley, were already experimenting with flight at that time. In 1896, a series of events would affect the brothers enough to make them pursue flight with serious intention. In May of that year, Langley reported the success of flying an unmanned, steam-powered model aircraft. Later on, Chanute also reported success is testing different types of gliders on the sand dunes near Lake Michigan. Then in August, headlines were made when Otto Lilienthal died while attempting a flight in his glider. Deeply affected by these events, Orrville and Wilbur gathered as much information as they could on flight and began their experimentation that year.

After drawing on the work of others, the Wright Brothers took a different path from their contemporaries and subsequently created the fundamental breakthrough that made flight possible. Their invention of the three-axis control allowed the pilot to steer the craft effectively and, most importantly, maintain its equilibrium. This method of control is still used today on all fixed-wing aircraft. Orville and Wilbur tested their technology as well as trained themselves to be pilots in a pasture now known as the Huffman Prairie Flying Field. Often frustrated by the lack of wind in the pasture, they looked for a place that had the necessary wind velocity and preferably soft landing terrain. Kitty Hawk, North Carolina, had what they needed and on December 17, 1903, they made the first controlled, powered, heavier-than-air human flight. Within two years, their flying machine would transform into the world's first practical, fixed-wing aircraft, taking its place in the history books forever and taking the rest of the world into the age of aviation.

LET THERE BE LIGHT

The Genius from Milan

You can't flip on a light, listen to music or watch a movie without touching on the legacy of one of the world's greatest genius inventors of the electrical age, Thomas Alva Edison. Born in Milan, Ohio in 1847, Thomas was the last of seven children. He attended school but did not do well. Edison ended up being home schooled by his mother.

The family moved to Port Huron, Michigan because of hard economic times. Life in Michigan wasn't much better, but it was where the wheel of destiny would start to turn for him. To help put food on the table, Edison sold candy and newspapers to passengers traveling on the trains running from Port Huron to Detroit. After snatching the train station manager's three-year-old child from the path of a runaway train, he was trained as a telegraph operator at the station as an offering of the manager's

gratitude. He was subsequently hired at Western Union where co-worker and fellow inventor Franklin Pope allowed the poverty-stricken Edison to live in his basement.

With his knowledge of the telegraph, Edison began inventing technology based on it. After inventing and then subsequently selling the stock market ticker, Edison was able to retire from his telegrapher job and fund his second career as an inventor. From that point on, the world was never the same. His inventions read like a laundry list of 19th and 20th century technology: the incandescent light bulb, the copy machine, the telephone carbon transmitter/microphone, the phonograph, the kinetoscope, the dictaphone, the radio, the electric lamp, the autograph printer, the cigar/cigarette lighter and even the tattoo gun. All in all, Edison would accumulate over 1500 patents worldwide, 1000 of them in the United States.

DID YOU  KNOW?

Edison was so fascinated with Morse code that he nicknamed his children "Dot" and "Dash."

OTHER NOTABLE INVENTORS

James Ritty (1837–1918)

Dayton saloon owner James Ritty had a good business going. Plenty of customers, plenty of help and enough profits to let a man sleep well at night. There was one problem, however. Some of his hired help had trouble keeping their hands out of the drawer where Ritty kept the money needed to run the business for that day. Frustrated, Ritty got an inspiration from watching a tool that counted the revolutions of the propeller on a steam ship. With the help of friend John Birch, Ritty created and patented the world's first cash register in 1883.

Alice Chatham (1908–89)

When Alice Chatham, a sculptor in Dayton, received a call from the U. S. Air Force, it wasn't because she was about to go into the military. It was because she was also about to become an inventor for the air force and NASA. At the military's request, Chatham designed a new kind of oxygen mask that would keep World War II pilots from fainting while in flight. In 1947, Chatham successfully designed a helmet just for test pilots. Again, her design worked beautifully—Chuck Yeager was wearing a Chatham original when he broke the sound barrier. The good word about her work must have spread, because NASA soon called her and asked if she could design a few things for them, too. She ended up creating a pressurized suit and full-head helmet and other equipment for the test chimps in the space program. Her designs for human use in space included a space bed, stretch-knit garments and various restraints and tethering devices to help deal with the pesky lack of gravity.

Charles Kettering (1876–1958)

Inventor Charles Kettering was born in Loudonville in 1876. He graduated from Ohio State University in mechanical and electrical engineering and went to work for the National Cash Register Company in Dayton. While there, he invented the world's first electronic cash register, among other things. He left NCR in 1909 to start his own company, the Dayton Engineering Laboratory Company (Delco) and it was there he would invent his most famous creation: the all-electric automobile starter. Automobiles at that time had to be hand cranked; it was a hard, dirty and often dangerous job. Kettering's new device erased all that. He made starting an automobile as simple as pushing a button. Over the years he would go on to invent an impressive list of items:

- Freon for refrigerators and air conditioners (in collaboration with Thomas Midgely Jr.)
- Safety glass
- Portable electric generator
- Four-wheel brakes
- Automatic transmission
- First synthetic aviation fuel
- Incubator for premature infants

He concluded his career as co-holder of more than 140 patents and honorary doctorates from 30 universities. A philanthropist as well, he co-founded the Sloan-Kettering Institute for Cancer Research in New York City.

DID YOU KNOW?

Kettering's residence in Dayton was the first air-conditioned home in the United States.

Charles M. Hall (1863–1914)

The next time you grab a can of pop, thank Charles M. Hall. This inventor from Thompson discovered a way to transform aluminum ore into aluminum by using electricity, revolutionizing a whole industry. Born in 1863 in Thompson, Hall decided while growing up that he would rather read than go outside and play. His father was a well-read minister and had several books which Hall would spend hours poring through. He especially enjoyed the college textbooks on chemistry his father had.

Hall graduated from Oberlin College in 1880 and began experimenting with aluminum, which was readily available in ore form but outlandishly expensive to extract. While working in his makeshift laboratory, he created a puddle of aluminum by passing electricity through a chunk of ore sitting in a special salt bath. At almost the exact same time, Frenchman Paul Héroult was discovering the same thing in France. Later, both men would be given credit and the method named the Hall-Héroult process. He sold the process to the Pittsburgh Reduction Company, which later changed its name to the Aluminum Company of America, also known as Alcoa. Because of his experimentation, Hall is credited with creating the first metal to attain widespread use since the prehistoric discovery of iron.

 Emil Fraze invented the pop-top can in Kettering.

OHIO IN SPACE

Ohio's Contributions to Space Technology

Maybe there's something in the water. Or perhaps it's because that Ohio is the birthplace of aviation. Whatever the influence is, it's a strong one—Ohio is home to 24 astronauts as well as being a major contributor to NASA's space program.

Here is the list of the famous Ohio men and women who walk the sky:

Neil A. Armstrong
Charles A. Bassett II
Kenneth D. Cameron
Nancy J. Currie
Donn F. Eisele
Michael J. Foreman
Michael L. Gernhardt
John H. Glenn, Jr.
Michael T. Good
Gregory J. Harbaugh
Karl G. Henize
Thomas J. Hennen
Terence T. Henricks
James A. Lovell, Jr.

G. David Low
Robert F. Overmyer
Ronald A. Parise, Ph.D.
Judith A. Resnik
Ronald M. Sega
Donald A. Thomas
Carl E. Walz
Mary E. Weber
Sunita L. Williams

First Man in Orbit

John H. Glenn, Jr., became the first American to orbit Earth when his Mercury Capsule Friendship 7 circled the globe in 1962. Born in Cambridge in 1921, Glenn was a fighter pilot during World War II and during the Korean War. After Korea, he became a test pilot and a project officer on a number of aircraft. During this time, he made the world's first supersonic transcontinental flight. He was selected for the space program in 1956, the oldest astronaut chosen at the time. In 1998, he became the oldest person to enter orbit while flying on board the space shuttle Discovery.

First Man on the Moon

Wapakoneta native Neil A. Armstrong was a test pilot for supersonic fighters and the X-15 rocket plane following World War II. Born in 1930, Neil was fascinated with flight from early childhood. His first space flight was in 1966 on Gemini 8, which he commanded. He, along with pilot David Scott, made history when they successfully completed the first manned docking of two spacecraft, a very tricky and dangerous maneuver. Armstrong's second and last space mission was on the Apollo 11 moon landing mission on July 20, 1969. As he planted the first human foot on the lunar surface, he left an imprint on the entire global audience, ushering us all into the next era of space exploration with the simple sentence "One small step for man, one giant leap for mankind."

DID YOU KNOW?

Neil Armstrong received his pilot's license before he received his driver's license.

Ohio's Challenger Connection

The world watched in horror on the morning of January 28, 1989 as the space shuttle Challenger disappeared in a large cloud of smoke, never to be seen again. Ohioans were especially grief-stricken, for one of their own was on board. The first Jewish woman and the second American woman in space, Judy Resnick, was born in Akron in 1949. Resnick was a scientist and electrical engineer. She joined the space program in 1978 and was on her second space mission when the Challenger explosion occurred.

Ohio, Supplier to the Stars

Russell Colley, a BF Goodrich engineer, designed NASA's first space suits in the early 1960s in Akron. Peter Van Schaik, who worked at the Wright-Patterson Air Force Base in Fairborn, created the life-support system and propulsion backpacks used during the Gemini space walks. Columbus engineer John Kraus designed the Helix antenna, a piece of equipment used on all communication satellites NASA sends into space.

DID YOU  KNOW?

The NASA Lewis Research Center in Cleveland is the only NASA facility outside the southern states. It houses the biggest refrigerated wind tunnel in the nation, where scientists can study how ice affects aviation.

MEDICAL INGENUITY

The Sabine Oral Polio Vaccine

The world first saw an effective polio vaccine in 1952, created by physician and researcher Dr. Jonas Salk. While Salk's vaccine was considered the first line of attack in the war against the disease, it would be the vaccine developed by Dr. Albert Sabine that would lead to complete victory over polio, leading physicians in 1994 to declare it eliminated from the U.S.

Working at Cincinnati Children's Hospital Medical Center, Dr. Albert Sabine created a vaccine that had three distinct benefits over other vaccines: it could be given by mouth instead of by injection; its live but weakened virus content gave a person both intestinal and whole body immunity (other vaccines delivered only bodily immunity, making it possible for a person to still be a carrier or transmitter of the virus); and finally it produced a lifelong immunity without the need for further booster shots or vaccinations.

Each year in the U.S., it is estimated that Dr. Sabine's discovery prevents 25,000 people from contracting the disease, saves 2000 people from dying and prevents 2500 from becoming completely disabled.

The Heimlich Maneuver

Cincinnati surgeon Henry J. Heimlich had an idea. If he could teach a simple technique to help ordinary people save choking and drowning victims, he could help "more people in a few weeks than in an entire lifetime as a surgeon in the operating room." He published his findings on the maneuver in 1974 and within a week a newspaper reported that someone had used it to save the life of a person who had been choking. Taught across the country in classes, this protocol has been credited for saving the lives of thousands.

Dentistry Developer

Arriving in Madison, Ohio, in 1823 to study medicine, Chapin Harris did not know then that he would eventually go down in the history books as one of the founding members of the dental profession in the U.S. as well as the father of American dental science and the pioneer of dental journalism.

A doctor first and then a dentist, Dr. Harris began contributing to medical literature in 1835. In 1840, he organized the first professional association of dentists called the American Society of Dental Surgeons and also founded as well as edited the world's first dental periodical, the *American Journal of Dental Science*. In the same year, he established the first dental school in the world, the Baltimore College of Dental Surgery, which would go on to graduate such notable dentists as James Taylor, founder of the Ohio College of Dental Surgery in Cincinnati and Wesley Sampler, the first dentist to extract a tooth from Abraham Lincoln.

COMMON CRIMES

Not Too Bad, But Not Too Good, Either

Ohio lands almost smack in the middle of average as far as state crime rankings are concerned, ranking 28th of the 50 states. Ohio criminals seem to prefer certain crimes. Ohio has higher rates of robbery (163 per 100,000 versus the national rate of 140 per 100,000) and theft (2429 per 100,000 versus the national rate of 2296 per 100,000). However, Ohio has lower rates of motor vehicle thefts, with 360 motor vehicle thefts per 100,000 people versus the national rate of 416. Apparently we covet our neighbor's goods, but don't need too many getaway vehicles.

Holding Steady

In 2007, Ohio was ranked the 23rd most dangerous state to live in, the same rank it achieved in 2006 and 2005. Unfortunately, according to a recent poll by Morgan Quitno Press, Youngstown and Cincinnati, with the ranks of 9 and 18 respectively, made the list of the top 25 most dangerous cities to live in. On the plus side, Ohio is ranked as the 37th most livable state.

NOTABLE CRIMINALS

The Beast from Bath

While forever pegged as the "Milwaukee Cannibal," serial killer Jeffrey Dahmer got his monstrous start in Ohio. His family moved to Bath in 1964, a village in suburban Summit County, when Dahmer was four. It was here that he would grow up and commit the first of what would eventually be 17 murders. Stephen Hicks, a hitchhiker, was picked up by Dahmer on June 28, 1978, and went back to his parents' house to have a few beers. After some time, Hicks attempted to leave but Dahmer picked up a barbell and hit him over the head and then strangled him. Dahmer first hid the body in the house's crawlspace but later fragmented the remains and spread them out over the backyard. After dropping out of college and receiving a dishonorable discharge from the army, Dahmer moved to Milwaukee, where he would commit the rest of his horrific murders until his arrest in 1991. He died in prison on November 28, 1994.

Prophet of Doom

Kirtland, located near Cleveland, welcomed a new family to their city in 1984. Jeffrey and Alice Lundgren and their four children moved there from San Diego and at first glance, they seemed to be a respectable, religious family. Jeffrey and his wife became tour guides for a local Mormon Temple museum and Jeffrey became a lay minister with the Reorganized Church of Jesus Christ of Latter-day Saints. Soon, however, it became apparent that the Lundgrens had worn out their welcome. Jeffrey became outspoken about his religious views, causing church officials concern. In 1987, both Jeffrey and Alice were fired from their jobs for stealing from the church.

Claiming that only he could interpret the holy scriptures, Jeffrey left the congregation with his family and two dozen followers and moved to a farm where he created his own religious cult. That same year, Dennis and Cheryl Avery, along with their three daughters, became followers of Lundgren and joined them at their farm. Two years later, Lundgren claimed the Avery family were "disloyal" and ordered his followers to help him with their murders. After digging a pit in the barn, Lundgren shot each family member and buried them. Lundgren and his followers left two days later and after an extensive nationwide manhunt, Lundgren was brought back to Cuyahoga County where he was convicted and sentenced to die. He was executed on October 24, 2006.

The Manson "Family"
Born in Cincinnati in 1934, rejected by his mother and spending the majority of his life either in reform schools or prison, Charles Manson would go down in history as one of the country's worst murderers. After his release in 1967, Manson moved to California in the hopes of starting a music career. After a lukewarm career in music, he started a commune-like group of people already on the fringe of society and began calling them "his family." He was known as the group's anti-Christ leader, commonly called "Death" or "The Devil."

In an attempt to start a race war as well as get back at those whom he thought had wronged him, Manson had his followers break into the home owned by a man who had refused Manson a record deal, and kill anyone who happened to be on the premises. On August 9, 1969, Sharon Tate, the pregnant wife of filmmaker Roman Polanski, Steven Parent, Wojciech Frykowski and American coffee heiress Abigail Folger were stabbed to death. The following night, Manson's "family," under his direction, killed Leno and Rosemary LaBianca in their Los Feliz home. Authorities arrested Manson and his followers shortly thereafter. After a seven-month trial, Manson and four of his followers were convicted and sentenced to life in prison in California, where they remain today.

Mass Murder on Easter Sunday

In 1975, James Ruppert decided he had had enough. Of what, no one knows for sure, but whatever it was, it motivated Ruppert to shoot the 11 family members gathered at his mother's home for Easter Sunday. The house on Walter Avenue in Hamilton, near Cincinnati, still stands as a solemn reminder of the country's largest family mass murder, with Rupert taking the lives of his mother, uncle, sister-in-law and eight nieces and nephews. After the shootings, James waited three hours before calling police and then calmly greeted their arrival by standing inside the front door amid the carnage. While the possibility of greediness regarding inheritance came to light during the trial, there was never a satisfactory answer as to why he did what he did. James Ruppert received dual life sentences in 1982 and is now serving time till his Easter Sundays run out.

DID YOU KNOW?

The movie *The Fugitive* starring Harrison Ford was loosely based on the story of Dr. Sam Sheppard, a physician from Bay Village, Ohio, and the highly controversial trial regarding the murder of his wife.

Pretty But Deadly

Having narrowly escaped the clutches of the FBI several times previously, Charles "Pretty Boy" Floyd similarly eluded the local authorities when he arrived in Ohio. Already famous for robbing more banks and stealing more money in 12 months than Jesse James did in 16 years, he and one of his partners in crime got caught in the middle of a bank holdup in Sylvania, Ohio. He was captured, tried and convicted but escaped while on his way to the Ohio prison to serve a 15-year sentence.

He would continue his crime spree for the next few years, terrorizing people in states across the Midwest. After being accused of killing an FBI agent along with four other men in the Kansas City Massacre in 1933, Pretty Boy Floyd slipped back into Ohio and hid among the farms and hills of East Liverpool, where he had spent time in the 1920s learning the art of bootlegging.

On October 22, 1934, the FBI was tipped off to his location and surrounded the barn where he was hiding. As Floyd ran for the woods for better cover, he was shot and killed. A marker, located between East Liverpool and Rogers, was erected to mark the spot where America's Public Enemy Number One died.

POPULAR OHIO SPORTS TEAMS

Love of Sports

Ohio loves its sports teams and is known for them. Few other states can beat the sports records of this state. Rich in sports history, Ohio is home to the birthplace of professional baseball (Cincinnati), and professional football (Canton), where the Football Hall of Fame is located. Ohio is also home to several other well-known professional teams. Cleveland has the Browns and the Indians; Cincinnati has the Bengals and the Reds; and Columbus...well, Columbus is a little different.

There's No Cure for Buckeye Fever

Columbus has a professional hockey team, the Columbus Blue Jackets. The city also has a professional soccer team, the Columbus Crew. It has a minor league baseball team called the Columbus Clippers. And the good people of Columbus do like their golf. But that's it. No professional basketball team. Just recently, they cautiously added a professional arena football team, the Columbus Destroyers. But still no National Football Leage team. In a city that's bigger than Cincinnati or Cleveland, that's unusual. So what's going on here?

Columbus and its surrounding suburbs are completely under the spell of a particular brand of fan madness called "Buckeye Fever," a truly zealous devotion to Ohio State University's football team, the Ohio State Buckeyes. While the rest of the state's population enthusiastically supports the Buckeyes, people in central Ohio are absolutely addicted to them. Residential bathrooms as well as other rooms are frequently decorated in scarlet and gray, the team's colors. Weddings are carefully planned so they do not conflict with scheduled games. Presents at baby showers often are little onesies with the Ohio State University logo on them. Coveted season tickets are passed down from one generation to the next. And when Ohio State plays its long time rival, Michigan, the streets are almost completely empty of traffic. Everyone is either home, at the Ohio State University or at a restaurant or bar, glued to the TV.

All of this zealous support leaves little room for a major league professional football (or baseball or basketball) team to call Columbus home. Buckeye fans are a monogamous breed and have a hard time imagining what life would be like if they had to share their passionate love with someone else. As far as they're concerned, the Ohio State Buckeyes are their first, and only, true love. Why change that?

The Legendary Coach: Woody Hayes

Buckeye fans, although devoted, are famously finicky about
their coaches, so much so that the school was dubbed the
"graveyard of college football coaches" before Woody Hayes'
arrival in 1951. Hayes satisfied the demands of Buckeye fans by
leading the team on to win 13 Big Ten titles, 5 national titles,
appearances in 8 Rose Bowls, 4 of them wins, and by coaching
58 All-American players, including 3 Heisman Trophy winners.
From 1968 to 1976, the Buckeyes lost only 13 games.
Unfortunately, Hayes' temper got the best of him during the
1978 Gator Bowl and he lost his job when punched a Clemson
University player for intercepting a pass, earning Hayes the
dubious title of "Most Unsportsmanlike-like Conduct Ever"
from CNN. Regardless of his temper, he was inducted into the
College Football Hall of Fame in 1983. When Hayes died in
1987, Columbus went into mourning—the flags in Columbus
flew at half-mast. Hayes' good friend, former president Richard
Nixon, delivered the eulogy at his funeral.

POPULAR SPORTS IN THE STATE

BASEBALL

Professional Team Snapshot: The Cincinnati Reds

☛ Major league baseball team based in Cincinnati

☛ Founded in 1866

☛ The team is in the Central Division of the National League

☛ Home ballpark: Great American Ball Park, Cincinnati

☛ Series Wins:

- 5 World Series Championships
- 1 American Association Championship
- 9 National League Championships
- 7 National League West Championships
- 1 National League Central Championship

☛ Team colors: red and white

Play Ball! (And Get Paid)

"Baseball should not be prostituted by salary payments." That's what the opposition said in 1869 when the president of the Red Stockings, now known as the Cincinnati Reds, decided to pay the players of his amateur baseball team. Needless to say, the sports world was shocked. Undeterred, president A.B. Champion went ahead and began the era of professional baseball. Reds captain George Wright received a salary of $1400 and wages for the rest of the team ranged from $600 to $1000. Not coincidentally, ticket prices jumped from 25 cents to 50 cents.

The 1869 Red Stockings created history in another way. The team created professional baseball's first winning streak at 92 games. Ironically, the Red Stockings were disbanded after 1870 because the owners couldn't afford to pay players' high salaries.

Pete Rose (b. 1941)

When one thinks about the Cincinnati Reds, the name Pete Rose always seems to come to mind. Nicknamed "Charlie Hustle" by former major league pitcher Whitey Ford because of his willingness to go the extra mile, Rose was named National League Rookie of the Year in 1963. Starting in 1964, this

Cincinnati native went on to bat .300 for the next nine years. Part of the "Big Red Machine," the nickname given to the team because of their dominance of the sport from 1972–76, Rose helped them win five division titles, three National League Pennants and two World Series. In 1975, *Time* magazine put Rose on the cover after awarding him the Sportsman of the Year award. Rose would go on to manage the Reds from 1984 to 1989.

Despite his achievements, Rose would never make into the Baseball Hall of Fame. Controversy erupted around him in 1989 when he was accused of betting on the team—both for and against. Rose was forced to agree to permanent ineligibility from baseball because of the validity of the charges. Denying it for years, he finally admitted in 2004 that he did indeed bet on the team.

Professional Team Snapshot: The Cleveland Indians

☛ Major league baseball team based in Cleveland

☛ Founded in 1901; had been playing 1889–99 under different league affiliations

☛ The team is in the Central Division of the American League

☛ Home ballpark: Jacobs Field

☛ Series Wins:

- 2 World Series Championships

- 5 American League Pennants

- 6 Central Division Titles

☛ Team colors: red and blue

What Was Your Name Again?

Cleveland was playing baseball before the sport was professionally organized. With the end of the Civil War in 1865, Cleveland's first team, The Forest City Club, was formed (Cleveland's nickname at that time was Forest City). In 1889 the team was renamed the Spiders because almost all the players were quite thin as well as being tall and gangly. When the team became one of the first four charter members of the American League, the moniker was changed to the more official-baseball-sounding name of the Blues, in reference to their uniform. Not content with that either, the players changed the name to the Broncos in 1902. In 1903, the team honored their player and manager Napoleon Lajoie by switching their name from the Broncos to the Naps. Finally, in 1915 the name of the Indians was taken as a way of honoring the first Native American player in the majors, Louis F. Sockalexis. He batted for the team from 1897 to 1899 when it was called the Spiders.

DID YOU  **KNOW?**

The Cleveland Press urged the Naps in 1908 to consider signing the first female semi-pro pitcher, Alta Weiss, by running a newspaper headline that said: "If The Nap Pitchers Can't Win Regularly, Why Not Sign Alta Weiss?" It didn't work.

Ohioans in the Baseball Hall of Fame
(birthplace and year inducted)

☛ Walter Alston, Darrtown, 1983

☛ Roger Bresnahan, Toledo, 1945

☛ Edward J. Delahanty, Cleveland, 1945

☛ William "Buck" Ewing, Massillon, 1939

☛ Roland "Rollie" Fingers, Steubenville, 1992

- Elmer Flick, Bedford, 1963

- Jesse J. "Pop" Haines, Clatyon, 1970

- Miller Huggins, Cincinnati, 1964

- Byron "Ban" Johnson, Norwalk, 1937

- Kennesaw Landis, Millville, 1944

- Richard "Rube" Marquard, Cleveland, 1971

- W. Branch Rickey, Stockdale, 1967

- George Sisler, Manchester, 1939

- Denton True "Cy" Young, Gilmore, 1937

- Ray Brown, Alger, 2006

- Mike Schmidt, Dayton, 1995

- Sol White, Bellaire, 2006

- Phil Niekro, Blaine, 1997

The Baseball Cyclone

Almost a hundred years later, there is one baseball player whose records time has yet to touch. Born in 1867 as Denton True Young, this Gilmore native would grow up to become the pitcher who would win the most games in Major League history, with 511 wins and 316 losses. In comparison, the second-highest scoring pitcher is Walter Johnson with 417 wins. Young's nickname "Cy" is short for "cyclone," a reference not only to his pitching style but also the effects of his pitches. While throwing for Canton, it was reported that "he so battered the wooden fence of the grandstand [with his pitches] that the Canton owner remarked it looked as if a cyclone had come through."

Cy's major league career started in 1890 with the Cleveland Spiders. In his debut, he allowed only three hits. He went on to pitch for St. Louis and Boston before retiring with Cleveland in 1911. He ended his career with 16, 20-game-winning seasons and 15, 30-game-winning seasons. Baseball honors him and his achievements with the Cy Young Award, a prestigious citation given each year to the best pitcher in baseball.

DID YOU KNOW?

Ohio native and entertainer extraordinaire Bob Hope owned a small share of stock in the Cleveland Indians and joined in the closing ceremonies of the Indians' final game in Cleveland Stadium.

BASKETBALL

Professional Team Snapshot: The Cleveland Cavaliers

☛ Major league basketball team based in Cincinnati

☛ Began playing in the National Basketball Association in 1970

☛ The team is in the Central Division of the Eastern Conference

☛ Arena: Quicken Arena (formally Gund)

☛ Season wins: 1 Division Title

☛ Team colors: wine, gold, navy, blue and white

The team got its name from a public contest where the citizens of Cleveland voted on the best sounding name for their team. Their choices were the Jays, the Cavaliers, the Foresters and the Presidents.

FOOTBALL

Professional Team Snapshot: The Cincinnati Bengals

☛ National League Football team based in Cincinnati

☛ Founded in 1967 in the American Football League; joined the National Football League in 1970

☛ The team is in the Northern Division of the American Football Conference of the National Football League

☛ Home field: Paul Brown Stadium, Cincinnati

☛ Championships: 2 Conference Championships, 6 Division Championships

☛ Team colors: Black, orange and white

Brown's the Name, Football's the Game

In 1967, an ownership group headed by Paul Brown was granted a franchise from the American Football League. As founder and former head coach of the Cleveland Browns from 1946–1962, Brown knew a thing or two about professional football. He named the team the Bengals as a nod toward another professional football team by the same name that had played for Cincinnati in the American Football League from 1937 to 1942. Brown also brought to the Bengals several innovations he had created during his time in Cleveland: he was the first coach to make the job a full-time, year-round position; the first to call plays from the sidelines by rotating players in and out; and the first to teach the game of football in a classroom setting. He coached the inaugural season of the Bengals in the University of Cincinnati's home field, Nippert Stadium. With financial help from the governor of Ohio, Riverfront Stadium was built in 1970 and the team played there until 1999. The new stadium is called Paul Brown Stadium and was named by Mike Brown, current owner of the Bengals and the son of Paul Brown.

Professional Team Snapshot: The Cleveland Browns

☛ National League Football team based in Cincinnati

☛ Founded in 1946 as a charter member of the AAFC

☛ The team is in the Northern division of the American Football Conference of the National Football League.

☛ Home field: Cleveland Browns Stadium

☛ Championship Wins:

- 4 AAFC Championships

- 4 NFL Championships

- 11 Conference Championships

- 13 Division Championships

☛ Team colors: seal brown, burnt orange and white

We're From Cleveland and We're Here To Stay

The team's origins began in 1946 when successful Cleveland business man Arthur "Mickey" McBride paid the $10,000 franchise fee for a professional football team. He approached Paul Brown, a football coach from northeastern Ohio, to come on board as the coach of his new professional football team. Brown was already well known in Ohio for football. As a high school football coach, he oversaw the Massillon Tigers to eight state football championships during his nine years there. In 1942, he led the Ohio State University Buckeyes to a national championship. Brown accepted the offer and the organization held a public contest to name the new team. The people chose the Panthers, but Brown objected since there was already a semi-pro team by that name. Another contest was held and the decision to name the team after the coach was the winner. Brown in turn coached the team through four hugely successful seasons. Their "perfect" year is considered 1948 because in that year, they won every game and had no ties.

In 1950, the Browns joined the National Football League and continued their winning streak by securing the championship title. Their fan base was secure and as the years progressed, the Browns experienced the usual ups and downs of any ordinary professional team. In 1995, however, a shocking announcement would turn the Browns' world on its ear: team owner Art Modell announced he was moving the team to Baltimore. The fans' opposition was intense; over 100 lawsuits were filed by fans, the City of Cleveland and many others. Congress even had hearings on the matter. Resolution finally came to the matter when Cleveland accepted a legal settlement that would keep the Browns legacy in Cleveland, including their name, colors, history, records, awards and archives. In February 1996, the National Football League announced that the team would be "deactivated" for three years and that a new stadium would be built for a new Cleveland Browns team. Modell would in turn be granted a new franchise for Baltimore, the Baltimore Ravens, retaining the current contracts of players and personnel. The fans were happy—starting in 1999, life was going to be orange and brown once again.

Professional Team Snapshot: The Columbus Destroyers

☛ Arena Football League team based in Columbus

☛ Founded in 1999 in Buffalo, New York; franchise moved to Columbus in 2004

☛ The team is in the Eastern division of the National Conference of the Arena Football League

☛ Home arena: Nationwide Arena

☛ Wild Card titles: 2

☛ Team colors: blue, black, white and red

The Destroyers called Columbus home after being purchased by John H. McConnell, the majority owner of the city's NHL team, the Columbus Blue Jackets. Wanting to ensure an attention-grabbing start to their first season, The Destroyers showcased former Ohio State University football coach Earle Bruce as their head coach and former two-time All American Ohio State University football player Chris Spielman as the front office manager. Spielman took over as head coach for the 2005 season but has since retired from the league. The Destroyers have been well received by their new fan base, with attendance records ranking among the highest in the league.

Ohioans in the Football Hall of Fame

(Birthplace and year inducted)

- Cliff Battles, Akron, 1968

- Jack Lambert, Manutua, 1990

- Paul Brown, Norwalk, 1967

- Joe Carr, Columbus, 1963

- Larry Csonka, Stow, 1987

- Len Dawson, Alliance, 1987

- Lou Groza, Martins Ferry, 1974

- Wilbur (Pete) Henry, Mansfield, 1963

- Clark Hinkle, Toronto, 1964

- Dante Lavelli, Hudson, 1975

- George McAfee, Ironton, 1966

- Mike Michalske, Cleveland, 1964

- Alan Page, Canton, 1988

- Roger Staubach, Cincinnati, 1985

- Paul Warfield, Warren, 1983

- Bill Willis, Columbus, 1977

- Chuck Noll, Cleveland, 1993

- Tom Mack, Cleveland, 1999

- Benny Friedman, Cleveland, 2005

- Dan Dierdorf, Canton, 1996

- Bob (Boomer) Brown, Cleveland, 2004

NOTABLE SPORTS FIGURES

John Heisman

John Heisman was the coach who set the standards in collegiate football. Born in Cleveland in 1869, Heisman influenced many of the characteristics seen in the game today. Heisman played college football at Brown University as well as the University of Pennsylvania. After college, he coached at Oberlin College, the University of Akron and Auburn College. During his coaching career, he developed the forward pass, the snap from center and the T and I formations, among others. Heisman retired from coaching and became the athletics director for the Downtown Athletic Club in Manhattan. It was here that the club began annually awarding what is now known as the Heisman Trophy, a coveted award that goes to the most outstanding collegiate football player in the U.S.

Archie Griffin

Born in Columbus in 1954, Griffin is the only college football player to have won the Heisman twice. Griffin is also the only player to start in four Rose Bowls.

Bobby Knight

Nicknamed "The General," Bobby Knight was born in Massillon in 1940. Knight has won more NCAA Division I men's basketball games than any other head coach. He is also one of the most controversial figures in college basketball because of his highly aggressive and sometimes combative behavior. Nonetheless, he has been praised for holding his team to high standards, both on and off the court. His players have a high graduation rate compared to other college basketball teams in the country.

Jesse Owens

Although born in Alabama in 1913, Jesse Owens' family moved to Cleveland when he was eight years old and he subsequently considered Ohio to be his home. Known as the "Buckeye Bullet," he attended Ohio State University and, as a track and field athlete, won a record eight straight individual NCAA championships.

Owens' greatest achievement would tie in with politics. He competed at the 1936 Olympics in Berlin, which Hitler had turned into a propaganda machine to promote the Nazi party and the theory of the superiority of the Aryan race. Owens, an African American, would go on to win four gold medals and the adoration of 110,000 Germans in the Olympic Stadium. During a time when African Americans did not have equal rights, Owens was allowed to stay in whites-only hotels and was granted access to many other whites-only facilities. Ironically, he was forced to ride the freight elevator in the Waldorf-Astoria hotel to attend a reception in his honor.

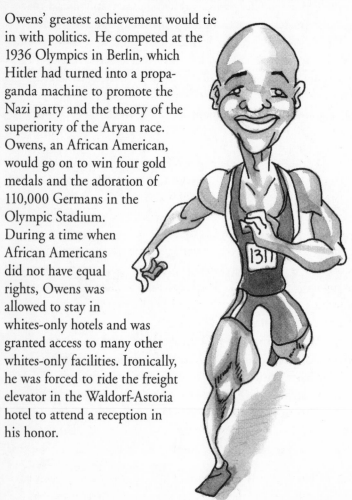

Jack Nicklaus

Born in Columbus in 1940, Nicklaus didn't pick up a golf club until the age of ten. It didn't seem to matter, though, because at the age of 12, he won the first of five straight Ohio State Junior titles and then won the Ohio State Open at the age of 16. He began his professional golf career in 1962 and is credited for turning the sport into the major spectator attraction it has become. Known as the "Golden Bear," he won the most majors of any professional golfer in his career, a total of 18 major championships. He was also the only player to win all four major championships three times in a career—a triple grand slam. Tiger Woods is the only other player who comes close to this record. Off the course, he is known for designing golf courses and for hosting the PGA Memorial Golf Tournament on his own course in Dublin, Ohio.

DID YOU  KNOW?

Rumor has it that the Memorial Golf Tournament is plagued by rain and bad weather because of a curse from a Wyandot Indian known as "Leatherlips." Living in the Dublin area at the time of the settlers' incursion, Leatherlips was so named because of ability to keep promises as well as being a kind and dignified example of his people. His native brothers, however, thought differently and accused him of being too friendly with the whites. They executed him on the banks of the Scioto River in 1810. Legend maintains that his final words took the form of a curse on the land that he once roamed, promising delays, disasters and general ill will toward any activity or people who happen to be in the vicinity.

Katie Smith

Regarded as the finest female basketball player in the history of the Big Ten conference, Katie Smith was born in 1974 into a family of athletes. In the small town of Logan where she grew up, she began playing basketball on the boys' team in the fifth grade. In high school she was named Gatorade Player of the Year her senior year. She attended Ohio State where, in her freshman year, she helped lead the Lady Buckeyes to a Big Ten Championship and NCAA title. In her senior year she was voted Big Ten Most Valued Player. Ohio State University honored her achievements by retiring her number, the first time this honor was bestowed on a female OSU athlete. Smith graduated from OSU and currently plays for the Women's National Basketball Association. In 2005, she became the first female American basketball player to score 5000 points in a professional career.

The only person to defeat notorious boxer Mike Tyson was Columbus native Buster Douglas. It was considered one of the most shocking upsets in modern sports history.

QUOTES, QUIPS AND CATCHY PHRASES

"We've got them."
–General George Custer of New Rumley,
on the Sioux attack at the Little Big Horn, 1876

"We have met the enemy and they are ours…"
–Oliver Hazard Perry to William Henry Harrison upon
his victory at the Battle of Lake Erie, 1813

"Now he belongs to the ages."
–Edwin M. Stanton, Cadiz lawyer and U.S. Secretary of War,
on the death of Lincoln, 1865

"All the news that's fit to print."
–Cincinnati's Adolph S. Ochs, publisher of the the *New York Times*, 1896

"I'm just a lucky slob from Ohio."
–Clark Gable, from Cadiz, 1940

"If you can't stand the heat, turn off the stove."
–Dayton city Commissioner Abner Orick, 1989

"The airplane stays up because it doesn't have time to fall."
–Wilbur Wright and Orville Wright, Dayton, 1905

"That's one small step for man; one giant leap for mankind."
–Neil Armstrong, Wapakoneta, setting foot on the moon, July 20, 1969

*"Genius is one percent inspiration
and ninety-nine percent perspiration."*
–Thomas Edison, Milan, 1932

"I will not accept if nominated and will not serve if elected."
–William Tecumseh Sherman, Lancaster, in response to the idea
of a Republican presidential nomination, 1884

"Hold the fort. I am coming."
–William Tecumseh Sherman to a besieged General John Corse, Georgia, 1864

"War is hell."
–William Tecumseh Sherman, in speech given in Columbus, 1880

"Good town. Good people. Good time."
–Prince Napoleon, commenting on Cleveland, 1861

*"Dayton is a place where inventors and innovators are treated
like baseball players."*
–New York image consultant, 1985

*"The Wright Brothers probably invented the airplane to have
a quick way out of town."*
–Tim Sullivan, the *Cincinnati Enquirer*, 1984

*"There goes one of those Georgia peaches. There's nothing
like that back in Ohio."*
–Bystander's observation of Scarlett O'Hara, *Gone With the Wind*, 1939

*"But hear me: a single twig breaks, but the bundle of twigs
is strong. Someday, I will embrace our brother tribes and draw
them into a bundle and together we will win back our country
from the whites."*
–Tecumseh, Shawnee Chief, 1810

ODDS AND ENDS

- Cleveland boasts America's first traffic light. It went into operation on August 5, 1914.

- Ohio is a leading producer of greenhouse and nursery plants.

- The popular television sit-com, *The Drew Cary Show*, was set in Cleveland.

- East Liverpool was the starting point of the United States Public Land Survey. The location was the area from which a rectangular-grid land survey system was established under the Ordinance of 1785. The survey provided for adminis-tration and subdivision of land in the Old Northwest Territory. The Ordinance stipulated that all public lands were to be divided into townships six miles square.

- The first full-time automobile service station was opened in 1899 in Ohio.

- In 1852 Ohio became the first state to enact laws protecting working women.

- East 105th Street and Euclid Avenue in Cleveland was the site of the first pedestrian button for the control of a traffic light. The boy chosen for the 1948 newsreel to demonstrate its operation was Louis Spronze.

- Oberlin College was the first interracial and coeducational college in the United States.

- Cleveland became the world's first city to be lighted electri-cally in 1879.

- Long jumper DeHart Hubbard was the first African American to earn an Olympic gold medal, at the 1924 Olympic games held in Paris. He set the record for long jumping.

TEN GOOD REASONS TO LIVE HERE

10. Ohio has an official state rock song. Sing "Hang On Sloopy" and you'll have an instant party.

9. Ohio's unique road maintenance system ensures a smooth drive—potholes are filled with asphalt in the summer and snow in the winter.

8. Ohio has the Rock and Roll Hall of Fame.

7. Ohio has variety. You can go north to the lake for boating and skiing, south to the river for dining and gambling, or to the middle of the state for shopping.

6. Ohioans have a laid back language. You can end your sentences with an unnecessary preposition and no one will mind. For example: "Where are my keys at?"

5. You're never more than 30 minutes away from a college or university, no matter where you are in Ohio. Seriously. Try it.

4. If you're hungry, you're in the right place. Agriculture and restaurants are big here! If you're not hungry, that's okay. The first chewing gum was made in Ohio and you can have that instead.

3. All you have to say is "Go Bucks!" anywhere in Ohio and you'll make instant friends.

2. Ohio is the roller coaster capital of the world!

1. Fickle about the weather? Then Ohio is definitely for you. If you don't like the weather, just wait a few minutes. It'll change.

ABOUT THE ILLUSTRATORS

Peter Tyler

Peter is a recent graduate of the Vancouver Film School visual art and design and classical animation programs. Although his ultimate passion is in filmmaking, he is also intent on developing his draftsmanship and storytelling, with the aim of using those skills in future filmic misadventures.

Roger Garcia

Roger Garcia lived in El Salvador until he was seven years old when his parents moved him to North America. Because of the language barrier, he had to find a way to communicate with other kids. That's when he discovered the art of tracing. It wasn't long before he mastered this highly skilled technique by age 14. He taught himself to paint and sculpt, and then in high school and college, Roger skipped class to hide in the art room all day in order to further explore his talent.

ABOUT THE AUTHORS

Alicia Adams

A true Buckeye, Alicia Adams was born in Ohio in 1967 and must have taken an immediate liking to the state because she has never left it. After earning a scholarship to Ohio State University, she spent two years living inside the famous horseshoe football stadium dormitory while earning her BA in English with an emphasis in creative writing and Latin. She decided to become a writer at the age of eight when she read about the world's youngest author in the *Guinness Book of World Records*. Alicia's articles have appeared in many publications including the *Christian Science Monitor*, *Single Parenting Magazine*, *Wee Ones Magazine* and many others. These days, Alicia is a freelance copywriter and enjoys time with her family and friends who all support her addiction to writing.

Lisa Wojna

Lisa Wojna, author of several nonfiction books, has worked in the community newspaper industry as a writer, journalist and editor, and has traveled the continent from the windy prairies to the wilds of the West Coast and east to the Atlantic. A trip to Ethiopia, however, was her most life-changing experience. Although writing and photography have been a central part of her life for as long as she can remember, it's the people behind every story that are her motivation and give her the most fulfillment.